THE POLITICS OF TORAH

THE POLITICS OF TORAH

THE JEWISH POLITICAL TRADITION AND THE FOUNDING OF AGUDAT ISRAEL

ALAN L. MITTLEMAN

STATE UNIVERSITY OF NEW YORK PRESS

Published by
State University of New York Press, Albany

For information, address State University of New York
Press, State University Plaza, Albany, N.Y., 12246

Production by E. Moore
Marketing by Bernadette LaManna

Library of Congress Cataloging-in-Publication Data

Mittleman, Alan.
    The politics of Torah : the Jewish political tradition and the
founding of Agudat Israel / Alan L. Mittleman.
        p.   cm.
    Includes bibliographical references and index.
    ISBN 0-7914-3077-4 (hc : acid-free). — ISBN 0-7914-3078-2 (pb :
acid-free)
    1. Judaism and politics. 2. Agudat Israel. 3. Orthodox Judaism-
-Political aspects. I. Title.
BM645.P64M58 1996
296.3'877—dc20   95-49366
                                                                CIP

10 9 8 7 6 5 4 3 2 1

This book is dedicated to my wife, Patti, who stood by me at every point, caring for our children, Ari and Joel, and for our home during the difficult time when I was in Germany. Her patience and fortitude are a wonder, and are admired by all who know her. May we go from strength to strength together.

CONTENTS

In the late twentieth century, religion and politics have become inextricable. Powerful fundamentalist movements, a term one must use with misgivings, have developed not only in Christianity and Islam, but in Buddhism and Hinduism as well. Something in the nature of modernity has produced an impressive, often worrisome realignment of religious forces. Contrary to earlier prognoses of inevitable secularization and the diminution of the public force of religion, our period daily witnesses struggles over the role of religion in modernized or modernizing societies that seem to wax rather than wane in intensity. One simply cannot afford to ignore the nexus of religion and politics.

The issues are interesting, however, not only because these so-called fundamentalist movements challenge the assumptions of the liberal West. They are interesting because, as William James might have put it, they derive from live and momentous options. The relation of religious faith and ethics to contemporary public life remains controversial. Not all the options, but many of the options remain open.

Since graduate school, I have been fascinated by the interaction of religion and politics. My concern has been both descriptive and normative. The ways of both Weber and Troeltsch, of the social scientist and the social scientifically-oriented theologian, interested me. As a graduate student, I was an avid reader of Reinhold Niebuhr and some time later

of such Catholic treatments of religion and political order as
are found in the writings of John Courtney Murray.
Illuminating as this literature was, however, I sought, especially for normative reasons, serious Jewish treatments of the
theme.

Much of what I discovered was not encouraging. Will
Herberg's writings transparently copied Niebuhr's. Much of
the literature was apologetic, testifying *ad absurdum* to the
harmony of Judaism and democracy without real probing of
either. Martin Buber, by contrast, presented himself as a model
of social theoretical and theological sophistication. I was not,
however, particularly drawn to either his dialogical philosophy
or his political utopianism. Antinomianism and responsible
political thought do not make good bedfellows.

While still in graduate school, it became increasingly
clear to me that Orthodox Jews were producing some of the
most interesting treatments of religion and public life. The
challenges to Jewish law (*halakha*) happily provided by the
State of Israel—I refer to the opportunities now available for
halakha to play an expanded public role in a sovereign polity—
evoked a sophisticated response from philosophically trained
halakhists such as Aaron Lichtenstein. Orthodox literati such
as Shimon Federbusch or the German Jewish thinker, Isaac
Breuer, confronted these challenges in their own idiom. It was
fascinating to see how Orthodox thinkers, who form in a certain way a permanent counter-culture vis-a-vis the modern
liberal West, negotiate their agreements and differences with
modernity. I looked increasingly to Orthodoxy as a subject
matter, that is, as an intellectual framework in which to study
the modern encounter of religion and culture, religion and
politics. Partly out of chance, partly out of choice, I looked to
German Orthodoxy for my case studies of those encounters.
German Jews, like German thinkers generally, took their positions to the logical limits. I found a clarity and a level of articulation in the German Jewish encounter with modernity that
was lacking elsewhere.

I probably would not have been able to contextualize
these Orthodox materials properly within the stream of his-

torical Jewish political experience had I not had the good fortune some years ago to come across the writings of Daniel Elazar. I have been even more fortunate to have had the opportunity of working with this remarkable scholar and thinker since. Professor Elazar provided a scholarly approach to the political dimension of the Jewish past (and, in light of the past, the present). He also, as a political philosopher, provides a way of bridging the world of religious texts and contemporary Jewish concerns. Much of what I try to accomplish in the present study was inspired by his way of thinking. At those points where I take issue with him, my aim has been to augment his perspective not to refute it. Although I do not follow him all of the time, I am convinced that his approach is not only sound, but compelling.

The present study is an exploration of the milieu, the "political culture," of a remarkable group of Orthodox Jews in Frankfurt am Main at the turn of the twentieth century. They wrestled with the conflicting demands of their allegiance to traditional Judaism with its implied concepts of sacred peoplehood and sacred polity and their Germanness, their bourgeois liberalism, their modernity. Out of this mix of impulses they created what they thought was the Torah made flesh on the stage of history: a renewed Jewish polity under the rule of God. Far from an Orthodox party or lobby, they believed that their organization, Agudat Israel, was the new historical form of *klal Israel*, the entire people of Israel. Exploring what beliefs of this magnitude meant to these historical subjects is the task of this study.

I knew when I began to research Agudat Israel that a political or social history of the movement, worthwhile as that would be, was not what I wanted to produce. As I was trained in the tradition of religion studies rather than history or social science, I wanted to produce a study that would put the religious dimension of their political activity in the foreground. This approach seemed necessary to me not only because of my own proclivities but because of the nature of the materials themselves. As we shall soon see, the Agudist texts mandated that the religious dimension be treated in its own integrity and not merely as an epiphenomenon. As I set about to write from this perspective, I found that I had to sort out methodological issues to a greater degree than I had imagined. Accordingly, this book dwells on conceptual problems more than some readers may find necessary. I can only hope that those looking for a more conventional historical treatment do not feel cheated by what they find here. At any rate, so little has been written about the earliest phase of Agudat Israel in Germany that I am sure any scholarly contribution, whatever its orientation, will be appreciated.

Many persons and institutions assisted me in the course of thinking through issues and doing research and writing. I am deeply grateful to Dan Elazar for his collegial support and friendship over the past few years. He has made following the Mishnah's advice to get a teacher for one's self easy. I am also grateful to my colleague and friend, Professor Johannes Brosseder of the University of Cologne. I had the very good fortune of working in his seminar during winter and spring, 1994, when I was an Alexander von Humboldt-Stiftung research fellow. Professor Brosseder practiced a hospitality of biblical proportions. My stay in Germany, never an easy experience for a Jew, was made exceptionally stimulating and hospitable by he and his wife, Gerlinde.

I also thank my good friends Dr. Stephan Eisel and Tina Albrecht-Eisel for their unfailing friendship (and translation advice). Allowing me to share their home in Bonn with them during my research in Germany was a great boon. My friend, Professor Robert Cohn and other colleagues, including the anonymous readers of State University of New York Press, reviewed the manuscript and enhanced my understanding of its potential and its problems.

Four institutions helped sponsor me in the course of preparing this study. Muhlenberg College, my academic home, awarded me its Class of 1932 Research Professorship during the 1993–1994 term which allowed me to have an entire year without teaching duties to devote to research. I thank its former and present academic deans, as well as my departmental colleagues, for their support. I also want to thank the Philip and Muriel Berman Center for Jewish Studies, and its director, for their sponsorship during several summers. They and Muhlenberg provided funds which assisted me in traveling to Jerusalem for symposia of the Jerusalem Center for Public Affairs. Those opportunities of collegiality with Israeli and other scholars broadened my perspective. It is also a pleasant duty to thank the Alexander von Humboldt-Stiftung for awarding me a research grant for 1994. Their professionalism defines what an academic foundation should be. I want to thank as well the staffs of the Wiener Library at Tel Aviv University, the Germania Judaica in Cologne, the Leo Baeck Institute in New York, the Orthodox Jewish Archives of America at the headquarters of Agudat Israel in New York, and the Jewish Museum of Frankfurt and its deputy director, Dr. Johannes Wachten. I gratefully acknowledge New York University Press and *The Jewish Political Studies Review* for their permission to use some brief portions of my earlier articles in this study.

A note about the cover art: the illustrations were taken from the pages of the newspaper Jacob Rosenheim published, *Der Israelit*. The art nouveau style, as well as the depiction of the female form, show an openness to the aesthetic norms of contemporary culture which would not be found among traditional Orthodox Jews today.

INTRODUCTION

In this study, we shall explore the origins of Agudat Israel, the first comprehensive, international, political movement of Orthodox Jews. Founded in 1912 in Katowice, formerly Kattowitz in the German province of Silesia, Agudat Israel represents, in an acute form, the confrontation of traditional Jewry with modernity. Its story sheds light on a process long of concern to social scientists, namely, the political development of traditional societies.

It is my belief, however, that Agudah's story should not *only* be read from the perspective of the political scientist, sociologist, or historian. The story must also be interpreted by the historian of religion. The founding of Agudat Israel, I suggest, constitutes a chapter in the history of Judaism. To embed the story in the "history of Judaism" and not only in the "history of the Jews" is apt because, from the perspective of our subjects, the German Agudists, their organization represented a crucial stage in the fulfilment of God's plan for Creation. They invested their political activity with metahistorical, cosmic significance. Agudah claimed to embody a sacred polity, with the Torah as its "organizing soul." The German Orthodox activists who founded the organization believed that the Torah was a constitution and that it was God's will that this constitution ground an actual Jewish polity. In their conception, political action became a sacred practice. Intercourse with the sacred occured in a political mode. There is no certain boundary between political experience and religious experience.

To take the perspective of one's subject seriously is a hallmark of contemporary religious studies. One wants to refrain as far as possible from imposing external categories on the materials one investigates. One wants to allow the data to suggest their own categorical contours. I have been led by this strategem in the present study. The profoundly religious impulse at work in the early Agudah movement suggests to me that the religious dimension of this phenomenon requires its own voice.

To take the perspective of one's subject seriously carries with it a train of problems. One does not only want to be a conduit for another's voice, that is, one wants not only to describe, but to interpret. Interpretation requires that one make judgments about data in terms of paradigms that are relatively external to the material at hand. To say that we are dealing with a religio-political phenomenon, or that, in this phenomenon politics and religion fuse, is to make an interpretive judgment through categorization. To complicate matters, it is not at all certain what "politics" or "religion" mean, especially when they are mutually implicated. Nonetheless, in order to use them with clarity, one must make some choices about how to constitute these categories. Without them, no light can be shed on the materials. The categories must be strong enough so that they do not merely posit a distinction without a difference. On the other hand, positing some essential, ontological content to each (such as "the Sacred" for Rudolf Otto or Mircea Eliade) seems precipitous. Minimally, we ought to avoid thinking of politics and religion as static hypostases which have mutually exclusive essences or unchanging contents. They are meaningful terms to the extent that they are useful ones. They are useful insofar as they aid in framing a question or guiding an inquiry.

Analyzing a movement where both terms present themselves as germane constitutes an interpretive problem with respect to any historical period. Where does politics leave off and religion begin? In an overtly religious age, people tend to view their actions in religious categories, thereby obscuring their political dimensions. We moderns, with our hermeneutics of suspicion by contrast, are very good at unmasking such "naive" obfuscations. But we run the risk, however, of veering too sharply in the opposite direction. We are apt to miss the genuinely religious aspects of the phenomena we investigate through positivistic reductions of one kind or another. When we turn to interpreting phenomena of our own time, where religion has become, in Thomas Luckmann's term, "invisible" (that is, religious phenomena have been driven underground where they persist unrecognized in social practices and rituals which appear secular on their face) we are prone to allow too much to become political. Empirically oriented as we are, especially in our role as historians, we assume that politics is the root category. Our methodology compels us to treat religious discourse as secondary, rhetorical, or derivative. Yet this evidently does damage to the way our historical subjects understood themselves. To the extent that historical men and women understood themselves to participate in a religious dimension of life which they thought genuine, our attempts to understand them must begin by taking this self-definition, this "definition of the situation," in Max Weber's phrase, into account.

Wilfred Cantwell Smith has long pointed out that the term "religion" underwent a profound transformation during the eighteenth century. Previously religion, when the term was used at all, had designated a dimension of inwardness or an ensemble of sacred practices understood to permeate the entirety of an individual or a culture's experience. But with increasing secularization, the term itself came to designate a discrete compartment of life and an identifiable system of beliefs. Religion, as a concept, got set against the concepts of art, philosophy, and politics. It moved from describing a quality attaching to all human thought and action to a department of life to be entered, left, chosen, or rejected at leisure. This demarcation and reification of the concept of religion has become part of the term's logical grammar, predisposing us to use it in particular and often unhelpful ways today.[1]

Thus, when we moderns use the term religion to mark off some parcel of human thought and action, we need to become more conscious of the ways in which we force the religiosity of premoderns onto our own Procrustean conceptual bed. This is particularly true with regard to "Judaism," itself a conceptual construct of early modernity. The intellectual deformation of an entire mode of life, both individual and communal, into a religion is precisely such a Procrustean bed.

A heightened suspicion about our own concept of religion, when applied to the problem of politics and religion, tempers our proclivity to see these terms as representing two different *kinds* of human experience. We ought rather to see them as constituting a continuum of experience. This is not to say that we can make no logical distinctions between them, but only that we must do so in a way that keeps the relation and the tension between the poles of the continuum alive. This certainly applies to our consideration of Jewish history.

Judaism, as a collective phenomenon, necessarily bridges the conceptual divide between politics and religion. The scriptural account of the giving of the Torah at Mt. Sinai is no less the story of the founding of a polity than it is the story of a theophany. Indeed, until early modernity both Jew and Gentile read the Bible in just this way: as a religious and political treatise. Hobbes, Spinoza, Locke, Kant, and numerous lesser contemporaries understood the Torah as the divine legislation of an actual polity. Moreover, the remnants of this polity, albeit without sovereignty, persist in the contemporary Jewish community.[2] Only with Jews such as Moses Mendelssohn, for whom Jewish civic integration was an overriding goal, did the political pole of Jewish self-understanding begin to weaken.[3] It is this political pole of Jewish self-representation that we must restore if we are to understand Agudat Israel. There is a line of continuity, at least in the minds of the Frankfurt Orthodox leaders who founded Agudah, between the sacred community assembled at Sinai and the sacred community reconstituted in Agudat Israel. How shall this assertion of continuity be understood? Is it, as a methodological cynic would assume, a convenient fiction—a species of false consciousness—or is it, as a methodological fideist would assume, simply the case that the God who led Israel to Sinai has led Orthodoxy back to the stage of history in 1912?[4]

Neither a historian nor a phenomenologist would presume to answer the latter question. Our inquiry must simply attend to viewing these utterances within the context of a living Jewish political tradition. Our working hypothesis, as the next chapter will detail, is that there is a substantive Jewish political tradition and that the Agudat Israel movement exemplifies its ideal-typical values and structures. The continuity that the Orthodox imagine between Sinai and Frankfurt is itself a fact of which interpretation must take account. Traditions live, at least in part, on the intentionality of traditionalists. The continuity of traditions over time is a matter of humans believing themselves to stand within the same stream of practice and belief. That Frankfurt experienced itself in the shadow of Sinai cannot be dismissed as "mere" imagination or, on a cynical reading, mere ideology. It is a moment in the ongoing stream of tradition, an instance of how traditions survive. Yet, having said this, we need not, of course, accept everything that traditionalists say about their traditions as the last word. The historian must determine when and how new elements break into the continuity of a tradition; how the tradition as a whole is reconfigured and transformed. We must inquire into what is ancient in Agudah and what is modern. How can we disentangle the contribution of distinctively modern influences from that which derives from the older Jewish political traditions of the medieval sacred community (kehillah) or, indeed, of the biblical community (edah)?

With questions such as these, we come to the dividing line between two different, but related types of inquiry. Up until now, we have tried to achieve greater clarity about how to approach an historical subject's own religious experience. That experience, of course, took place within the context of an external, historical situation. We must inquire both into the nature and structure of the Agudist experience of religion and politics, and into the historical conditions under which that experience occured. To an overview of those conditions, to be deepened in subsequent chapters, we now turn.

The founders of Agudat Israel (literally, the *band* or *union* of Israel) were, on the one hand, westernized German Orthodox Jews and, on the other, eastern European traditionalists.[5] Although they shared a belief in the revealed and sacred character of Jewish law and a commitment to live according to its dictates, the founders were divided by culture and by their experiences of modernization. The Westerners were farther along on the path of modernization and acculturation than were the Easterners. The Orthodox graduates of German universities and of Lithuanian yeshivot did not, literally, speak a common language.[6]

Different historical forces drove these groups to participate in a common project of political development. Given their very different cultures, their attitudes toward their project differed dramatically.

For the eastern traditionalists, the formation of Agudat Israel represented a case of political development in which the creation of new political institutions and structures rose out of a matrix of traditional institutions which were no longer able to cope with changing conditions. As is typical of such political development, the emergence of modern political structures emphasized mass participation and confidence in their capacity to direct social and economic change.[7] Agudah in the East represents therefore a modernizing, implicitly secularizing dynamic. It implies the inability of traditional ad hoc means of political activity, such as *shtadlanut* (intercession with the ruling powers), to respond to the challenges of the modern state and society, as well as the inadequacy of traditional religious authority to counter the inroads of secularizing Jewish movements such as Zionism and socialism. Thus, Alfred Döblin, in his memoir of Jewish Poland, quotes a Zionist who observed: "It is a sign of the decrease of clericalism that Orthodox Jews have had to form a party."[8]

Deeply distrustful of political development as a sign of the new, which was "forbidden by the Torah," the heads of Lithuanian yeshivot and hasidic dynasties nonetheless validated the Agudah movement as a purely defensive strategem.

Their challenge was to exploit political development and activity for legitimate purposes while containing the subversive, secularizing potential of such activity. This meant, among other things, rejecting any importation of the Western religious synthesis ("*Torah im derekh eretz*": Orthodoxy cum *Kultur*) of the German Jews. The Easterners wanted the benefits of organization, without the hazards of westernization.

For the German Jews, the main subjects of this study, political development also represented a modernization process. Crucially, however, it also signified a movement of reaction against several generations of modernization. Agudah in the West represents a pendulum swing toward the articulation of a coherent conservatism which was set in motion by the forces of liberal, bourgeois modernity. As they were farther removed from the ghetto than their eastern counterparts, the German Jews' impulse toward political, communal activism arose from a different set of needs. They sought in politics an antidote to their distance from the ghetto's integral social and religious cosmos. They sought, ultimately, an avenue of religious experience; an entrance to processes of repair and salvation. Agudah was conceived as a way of employing a distinctly modern, rational instrument—a political movement—in order to achieve a distinctly nonmodern end: a sacred polity. While the eastern traditionalists allowed for political development in order to keep modernity at bay, the German Jews thought to sanctify politics in order to seek redemption. The Easterners, precisely while differentiating and rationalizing politics, tried to hold to a modest, pragmatic attitude toward political activity. The Westerners, on the other hand, invested the political realm with cosmic symbolic weight and purpose. While these divergent attitudes were equally balanced in the beginning, the eastern view prevailed as the century progressed. The observer of Agudat Israel today, in its role of political party in Israel and interest group in the United States, would find this theologically charged description of Agudat Israel rather surprising.[9]

For the eastern traditionalists, rational (as opposed to adventitious) political activism was suspect. Since the loss of political independence in antiquity, Jews believed that they were powerless to effect radical changes in their condition of exile.[10] Dependent upon the gentile powers, they awaited the ultimate divine redemption, which alone would alter the course of history. Political activity was directed toward the ordering of the community internally and toward external interventions with the gentile powers in order to maintain or, if possible, improve the status quo. Political action without sovereignty over a territory was necessarily restricted. Nonetheless, Jews enjoyed considerable internal autonomy throughout the Middle Ages. This was steadily eroded in both the East and the West by the growth of the modern state. The eastern traditionalists' conception of political activity reflected medieval concerns. It was minimalistic and practical. Political activity was a holding action designed to buy time while the messiah tarried.

This premodern attitude continued to prevail among the traditional leadership in the East into the early twentieth century. The idea that history is dynamic, that Jews can alter their destiny in a fundamental way through political action remained, for the vast majority of rabbinic leadership, foreign and subversive. Even more subversive however was the ever-growing intrusion of forces, such as Zionism and socialism which held to a dynamic view of history, into the traditional communities. The founding of a religious Zionist movement (Mizrachi) in 1902 underscored the proximity and urgency of the threat. Many traditional Jews, though committed to practical efforts in the land of Israel (Hibbat Zion) rejected Zionism in its modern form as irreconcilable with political quietism.

Paradoxically however, some rabbinic leaders felt that Zionism and socialism had to be countered with their own weapons, namely organized, *rational*, political action conducted by a supra-local body at a level of organizational competence and complexity commensurate with that of the secular opposition. The strengthening of traditional institutions and values, as well as the representation of traditional interests in the political sphere required the development of political structures out of the traditional religio-social background. Political action had to become rational.

Yet despite cognizance of the threat of encroaching modernity, other rabbinic leaders viewed "politicization as a betrayal of the religious tradition that Orthodox politicians would be defending."[11] They contended that to become political meant to abandon the absolutist stance of the tradition. An Orthodox political party would have to engage in bargaining, compromise, and parliamentary cooperation. How could Orthodox Jews, whose only reason for being was an absolute, unconditionally true Torah project themselves, in the name of that Torah, into a parliamentary political culture? These traditionalists sensed the inherent, secularizing dynamic of political development. The counter-argument was that the political representation of Orthodox interests was not discontinuous with the pragmatic tradition of *shtadlanut*, of statesman-like representation of the community's interest to the powers that be.[12] For this latter group, primarily the Gerer Hasidim and heads of Lithuanian yeshivot, *shtadlanut* served to legitimate the new political structure as well as to serve as a norm for political action. Here we see a typical example of the persistence of a traditional element—a norm and a practice, that is, politics as *shtadlanut*—enduring under the radically changed conditions of modern parliamentary politics.

The event that spurred the creation of Agudah was the departure, in 1911, of some religious Zionists from the 10th Zionist Congress. The religious Zionist movement, which had been rejected by the vast majority of traditional leaders in Eastern Europe as an unacceptable syncretism, had an uneasy relationship with the Zionist movement as a whole. As long as Zionism focused on the practical activity of colonization a few Orthodox leaders were willing to go along. In 1911, however, the Zionist Congress decided to sponsor cultural and educational work along the lines of the predominant nationalist and secularist ideology. Some Mizrachi delegates walked out. This group soon made common cause with the anti-Zionist traditionalists who were developing the ground work for Agudat Israel.

Although organized in 1912, Agudat Israel did not become fully functional until after the First World War. By the 1920s, Agudat Israel became the second strongest political party among Jews in Poland representing major cities like Warsaw and Lodz in the Sejm. Its politics were minimalist. Agudah professed Polish patriotism, assumed the good will of the gentile majority, and sought to improve Jewish rights within the existing political framework. That the Polish branch of Agudah conceived of modern parliamentary politics as an extension of medieval *shtadlanut* was often noted by its Zionist, socialist and nationalist opponents.[13] Agudist party organizations also existed in Hungary, Czechoslovakia, and Lithuania. It was most successful in Poland, owing to the support of a large Hasidic group, the dynasty of Gur.

While traditionalists in the East were willing to participate in a political movement, it was western Orthodoxy that had the know-how and resources to create one. Western Orthodox Jews were highly modernized. In Germany, where the idea of Agudah originated, the Orthodox were a minority community within German Jewry. This minority was, furthermore, divided against itself. Although virtually all German Orthodox Jews, like their liberal brethren, affirmed German culture and the Empire, they divided over their attitudes toward the non-Orthodox Jewish majority.

Most of German Orthodoxy cooperated with non-Orthodox Jews. The majority of Orthodox rabbis and synagogues participated in common communal structures (*Einheitsgemeinden*) which provided for separate services to accomodate Orthodox needs. Some Orthodox, however, believed the dominant Liberal Judaism to be a heresy of such magnitude that even the tacit acknowledgment which participation in common structures signified was unacceptable. Under the leadership of Samson Raphael Hirsch (1808–1888), these Jews won the legal right in 1876 to secede from the general Jewish community and form their own separatist structures (*Austrittsgemeinden*). For Hirsch and some (but not many) others, separatism came to be understood as an absolute demand of the Torah.[14]

The ideologues of separatism viewed separatist communities as restorations of the presumably archetypal polity of

Judaism and hence as the sole valid form of Jewish community.[15] Although the manner of worship and conduct of life
within Frankfurt's or Berlin's separatist community did not differ from that of the Orthodox in unified communities, the mere
existence of independent entities seemed to fulfil a crucial principle of the Torah. The Torah was viewed, in part, as a constitution. Its divine Giver was the head of state. Acknowledgment
of the sole sovereignty of God was made, on the individual
level, by a life of fidelity to the commandments. But how, in the
absence of Davidic monarch, holy land and Sanhedrin could
divine sovereignty be expressed on the communal level? The
answer of the Orthodox separatists took a negative form: by
nonrecognition of the communal structures of those who deviate from the Torah. While they might personally be acknowledged as sinning brethren and therefore merit dialogue and care,
their communities must be seen as institutionalized rebellion
against divine law. The separatist communities, as stubborn
repositories of the idea of Divine/Torah sovereignty resisted
modern principles of political organization, such as democratic
pluralism. To live in a society governed by Torah required the
rejection of other governing principles, of other constitutions.
Clearly, separatist Orthodoxy had a distinctly political conception of Jewish life.[16] This political dimension is inseparable from
their religious self-understanding.

The idea of Agudat Israel was developed in the discussions of the Frankfurt separatist group from 1905 on. On one
level, Agudat Israel might be seen as an extension and further
rationalization of that community's earlier political activism
(e.g., Samson Raphael Hirsch's *Freie Vereinigung für die
Interessen des Orthodoxen Judentums* or the *Kollel Holland
und Deutschland*). In chapter 3, we shall trace the connections between the two organizations. On another level, however, it ought to be seen as an attempt to provide a positive
content to the urge to live in a Torah-governed society, that is,
to fully implement the Torah-constitution. Thus, while the
eastern Jewish interest in a political movement was defensive, antimodern, and pragmatic, the German interest was
utopian, restorative and messianic.

Whence this driving passion to create a Torah-society in Frankfurt and Berlin, and from thence to renew the Jewish polity in a theocratic mode for the whole of Jewry?[17] It is remarkable that the German Orthodox nurtured such dreams, while the eastern Jews contented themselves with a more pragmatic politics. To answer this question, we have to get at the bases of German Jewish identity in general, and Orthodox identity in particular. This identity was built on two pillars: *Bildung*, that is, the acquisition of German culture and *Konfession*, that is, the transformation of Jewishness into an entirely religious phenomenon fully compatible with German nationality.

The uniquely hybridized German-Jewish identity which both Orthodox and Reform Jews shared was a product of the social and cultural transformation of both the German and the Jewish societies in the late eighteenth and nineteenth centuries. At the end of the eighteenth century, the German states went through a process of modernization which included increasing rationalization of administration and economy, industrialization, urbanization and the emergence of an educated bourgeoisie (*Bildungsbürgertum*) to staff the expanding state bureaucracies. The educated bourgeoisie, although essentially created by the monarchies of the German states to aid in the consolidation of their power, eventually came to challenge their control of politics in the name of liberalism.

A key component of the German version of liberalism was the Enlightenment concept of *Bildung*.[18] *Bildung* referred to a process of autonomous self-formation under the guidance of practical, that is, moral, reason. Although rooted in religious categories of Lutheran pietism, Enlightenment *Bildung* was a secular ideal. Its root category was the individual as a locus of moral cultivation and development. Each individual was capable of achieving an harmonious, ethically and aesthetically developed personality. The process was initiated and advanced through education. The role of the State was to ensure that individuals possessed enough freedom to pursue their ontological-moral destiny and to offer them the kind of humanistic education by which they could perfect it. In

German thought, the State became the guarantor of freedom and the tutor for the moral self-development of the citizen. *Bildung* and paternalistic absolutism were highly compatible in the German Enlightenment.

Bildung was more than the concern of an intellectual elite. It became the ideology of the rising middle classes in the Enlightenment period, reflecting, at the level of Weltanschauung, their struggle for a more open, meritocratic society as against the ancient claims of estates, guilds, and monarchy. Against this background, one can understand the interest of the educated bourgeoisie in the Emancipation of the Jews. Given their stated commitment to the possibility of the moral improvement of the individual, whatever his background or religion, the educated bourgeoisie saw in Jewish emancipation the test case for their theory of a new society.

The German version of the Emancipation offered Jews rights in exchange for their moral self-development, indeed, transformation. While the French demanded that the Jews become Frenchmen, the German sponsors of emancipation demanded that the Jews become educated. German Jews responded with programs for personal and cultural transformation: Haskalah in the first phase of the Emancipation and Wissenschaft des Judentums in the second. As is clear in Moses Mendelssohn and the Haskalah writers, German Jews, desirous of achieving equality in German society, emphasized *Bildung* as their "passport to European civilization." In this way, an Enlightenment philosophical ideal compounded with a political ideology of liberalism became an enduring component of German-Jewish self-definition.

According to George Mosse, "the centrality of the ideal of Bildung in German-Jewish consciousness must be understood from the very beginning—it was . . . fundamental to the search for a new Jewish identity after emancipation. The concept of Bildung became for many Jews synonymous with their Jewishness, especially after the end of the nineteenth century, when most Germans themselves had distorted the original concept beyond recognition."[19] The Jews' modern identity thus depended upon an Enlightenment synthesis emphasizing rationality, education, middle-class mannerliness, and liberal politics. As Germany came to abandon many of these ideals under pressure from exclusivistic nationalism, anti-Semitism and irrationalism, Jews became the principle tradents of the Enlightenment tradition. Jews continued to believe that forming themselves under the imprint of German classical culture and holding that culture as a sacred part of their own deepest consciousness and character (*deutsche Gesinnung*) would ensure their acceptance as full-fledged members of the German Volk. They could not abandon *Bildung* without abandoning themselves. The Germans, however, progressively abandoned the Enlightenment and its liberal, *Bildung*-contingent concept of social equality in favor of more deeply rooted tribalistic and eventually racial criteria of social acceptability. German Jews, by contrast, clung to the Enlightenment until the end, thinking themselves thereby the last true Germans. In 1933, as the Nazis excluded Jews from German cultural life, the newly formed Jüdische Kulturbund chose Lessing's classic depiction of *Bildung*, Nathan the Wise, as its first production.[20]

Another aspect of the Emancipation era transformation of Judaism and the Jews was confessionalization: the metamorphosis of Jewish national consciousness into a purely "religious," that is creedal, phenomenon. Beginning with Moses Mendelssohn and, in the nineteenth century, with the nascent Reform movement, Jews radically deemphasized Jewish nationality and presented Judaism as a confessional variant on the pan-human Enlightenment "religion of reason." Gabriel Riesser (1806–1863), the leading Jewish proponent of emancipation in the Vormärz and the second vice-president of the Frankfurt Assembly in the 1848 revolution maintained that the attribution of separate nationality to Jews was a "fable." A nation required: "land, language, a constitution, political power, and independence; or the struggle for these requirements. These elements are the precondition of a nation; where all of them were lacking, as in the case of the Jews, the foundation for a nation was non-existent."[21] Similarly, Moritz Lazarus, another leading Jewish spokesman of the 19th century made nationality contingent on subjectivity, to feel one-self a German is to be a German: "My people are those whom I recognize as my people, those whom I call mine, those to whom I am tied forever . . . We are German, nothing but Germans, when we talk about the concept of nationality we belong to only one nation, the German one."[22] With the self-imposed elimination of Jewish nationality, Judaism narrowed to a tenuously contingent religious reality. Keeping in mind what we noted earlier about the compartmentalization of the concept of religion, we can see how Jews might believe them-selves to be fully German since their "religion," depoliticized and denatured into a creed was, at any rate, nothing more than a philosophical system of ideas (albeit with related acts and symbols which concretized the ideas). Of course, the problem of residual nationhood, ethnicity, did remain. Hermann Cohen, a leading German-Jewish philosopher who argued for the spiritual identity of Judaism and Germanness (conceived as highly essentialistic ideals), regretted that Jews did not yet have Germanic physical features. He urged the Germans to "Have patience!"[23]

Orthodox Jews operated within this self-definitional framework no less than did liberal Jews. As to the first crite-rion, the affirmation of *Bildung,* one need only consider the articulation of neo-Orthodox identity accomplished by Samson Raphael Hirsch (1808–1888) and Esriel Hildesheimer (1820–1899) in the nineteenth century. Both embraced the emancipation, affirmed German *Kultur* and modernized Jewish primary, secondary, and rabbinical education. Hirschian concepts of "Torah im derekh eretz," and "Mensch-Yisroel" are components of a *Bildungsideologie* that facilitated the maintenance of a peculiarly German Orthodox identity well into the twentieth century. Similarly, Hildesheimer's creation of a modern, yet Orthodox, rabbinical seminary illustrates both the importance of university educated rabbis for German Orthodoxy and the underlying Mendelssohnian optimism that modern learning and traditional faith are fully compatible.

The second criterion, confessionalization, presents a more complex picture. German Orthodox Jews were a largely middle-class, successfully assimilated, patriotic group. They affirmed and consumed (although did not produce) German culture to the same degree as Reform Jews. Orthodox Jews did not go as far as Reform Jews however in either the denial of Jewish nationality or in the rhetoric of German-Jewish spiritual identity.[24] An analysis of a sermon by Samson Raphael Hirsch reveals both the overlap and the exceptionalism of the Orthodox vis a vis the German Jewish majority.

Hirsch's 1855 sermon for Tisha b'Av takes its point of departure in a critique of a proposal by a radical Reform rabbi of the previous generation that the fast ought to be abolished insofar as mourning for Jerusalem implied "treason and enmity towards the State and Fatherland. He called on his dismayed congregation," Hirsch continued, "to show by means of a festal celebration their repudiation of the out-of-date yearning for Palestine, and to give proof of their patriotic attachment to the Fatherland in which they lived and worked."[25] Hirsch expresses his undisguised contempt for this position and then precedes to argue why real mourning is still necessary.

In Hirsch's view, it is no less a duty of the emancipated Jew to remember and mourn for Zion than for the enslaved and oppressed Jew. A Jew has eternally binding duties regardless of his historical circumstances. If emancipated Jews do not mourn for Zion, then they mock all the martyred Jews of the past who have done so. Such an appeal to sacred memory is not surprising. What is surprising is the rhetorical twist Hirsch puts to the theme of Jewish martyrdom:

> The heavier the oppression, the blinder the hatred, the greater appeared to them to be the mitzvah, the more brilliant the kiddush hashem, when the opportunity was afforded to them of sanctifying God's name by promoting the welfare of the stepmotherly state. With heartfelt and genuine affection they clung to the soil on which their cradles had been rocked, on which they had greeted the first laughter of their children, which, however grim and forbidding without, had kept intact for them the homes

where they could enjoy their sweet and God-fearing life. Only with a struggle, only under the stress of extreme need, did they bring themselves to wander away to a strange country; with deep and strong love they clung to the land of their birth and of the graves of their ancestors; but they looked with equally strong and deep yearning towards Palestine.[26]

Hirsch thus argues that in earlier epochs of persecution, Jews were nonetheless enthusiastic patriots of their native lands. This praise of loyalty to fatherland, conjoined with love of Zion, must be taken more as an attestation of Hirsch's own patriotism than as an historical description of premodern Jewish attitudes. Hirsch's extraordinary devotion to Germany and later to the Kaiserreich were graced with the status of mitzvah in his 1837 code, *Horeb*.[27] The elevation of love of *Vaterland* to a "duty of the heart" shows the extent to which an interiorized Germanness (*deutsche Gesinnung*) was crucial for Hirsch.

While not rejecting, as Reform Jews did, the status of a separate Jewish nationality, Hirsch qualifies these concepts in order to accord with the modern framework of German-Jewish identity. Hirsch believes that Jews are a nation, but a *Religionsnation*: a nation of a wholly unique, in fact, divine type. Providence has scattered this unique "nation" among the peoples in order to mix with them in freedom (an intention the nations have at last acknowledged), imbibe their cultures and sanctify them before God. Jews transform the human to the holy: "Mensch-Yisroel" indicates this process of sacral transformation. By living among the nations and assimilating their manners and culture, Israel becomes a conduit for relating the merely human to the Torah. The Jew is rooted in the human (the *Mensch* aspect of his being) and proceeds toward the holy (the *Yisroel* aspect). This mission on behalf of the world is accomplished through the harmonious perfecting, under the aegis of a divine education, of both the individual Jew and of the nation. The Enlightenment-oriented aesthetic and moralistic interpretation of the commandments in *Horeb* is unmistakable. The less attenuated concept of nationalism the tradition conserves requires the messianic age for its expression. Until that time, Orthodox Jews are secure in saying "We are Germans."

Orthodox Jews, guided by Samson Raphael Hirsch, successfully assimilated into the German middle classes. Yet, while they retained traditional religious observance, they lost much of the traditional, preemancipatory outlook. Consequently, there was always a sense of distance from the past, of loss, occasionally, of malaise. The pure, sacred and separatist community was an attempt to recreate what was imagined to be the traditional communal structure. Yet, insofar as its principle was wholly negative, it showed how attenuated the religious lifeworld and the Jewish political tradition had become. While mindful of "talis and tefillin," Orthodox minds were shaped by Goethe and Lessing no less than those of other educated German Jews. The Orthodox brooded about the "Torah's demand for totality" (*Totalitätsanspruch der Torah*) and the fact that their Jewishness defined, at best, limited dimensions of their lives rather than the whole of life (*Lebenstotalität*).[28] While the Eastern Jews sought to ward off modernity, even at the cost of grasping a double-edged sword, the German Jews sought to recover from modernity the Jewishness they had lost through a century of adaptations. They wanted to move beyond a synthesis of Judaism and modernity into a totalistic assertion of Jewish being. Thus, Orthodoxy was a conservative movement in Karl Mannheim's sense: a deliberate reaction to liberal modernity which, inevitably, continued to bear some of the traits of both the liberalism and the modernity out of which it arose.

Political activity is a response, for German Orthodoxy, to what Weber called the "disenchantment of the world."[29] The lifeworld of the Orthodox, no less than the Liberal or secular German Jew had long lost the dimension of miracle and mystery. Orthodoxy embraced a post-Kantian theology wherein life according to the commandments was understood as a means of moral training. By the nineteenth century, Judaism had become, for Orthodox and Liberal Jew alike, a religion within the limits of reason alone. Ethics replaced the old tradition of mysticism as the fundamental legitimation of the religious life. One response to the intuition of disenchantment was to take a rational/technical, that is, disenchanted medium such as politics and invest it with transcendent significance. Politics became a medium of sanctification, a form of theurgy. It not only alters historical states of affairs, it restructures cosmic order, that is, it transforms disorder into order. The cosmic disorder is evidenced by Israel's diaspora situation. Political activism establishes a symbolic center around which the scattered tribes of Israel may regroup. The mere fact of this symbolic center—that is, the cluster of committees which make up the Agudah—reestablishes the divine reign over Israel, and consequently over history.

Convictions of this order pervade the writings of the Agudist ideologues of Frankfurt. For Jacob Rosenheim (1870–1965), the principal architect of Agudat Israel and its president for decades, the founding of the Agudah constitutes an act of historical and cosmic moment. The name itself, in Rosenheim's view, is redolent with meaning. The Hebrew term *agudah*, deriving from the verbal root to bind, means "band" or "association." Thus the name of the movement, the "band of Israel," implies both the actualized result of the process of binding and the process itself. A principal citation of the word *agudah*, noted by Rosenheim, occurs in one of the most solemn and messianic prayers of the Jewish New Year service. The prayer envisions a future epoch in which all creatures will become full of the "fear of the Lord," recognizing Him as Creator and Sovereign. They will become "one band" (*agudah ahat*) to do His will. Short of this complete cosmic transformation, Israel is the present locus of fear of the Lord and acknowledgement of His sovereignty. The name of the movement, therefore, signifies an incipient messianic dynamic. The binding together of Israel under the sovereignty of God anticipates and promotes the universal redemption.

In Jacob Rosenheim's view, Israel was once such a unity. The experience of Emancipation however shattered western Jewry into various trends and diminished its ties with eastern

Jewry. The function of an Orthodox world organization is restorative. It must give concrete historical expression to the spiritual reality of *klal Israel*: the transcendent (as well as transcendental) unity of Israel. Conscious of the enormous historical import of the project, Rosenheim asserted that,

> Agudat Israel is the first historical attempt, after the fall of the Jewish State, to regenerate the Jewish People— despite its diaspora in all lands—in the form of a living organism so that its anarchic masses can be ordered and assembled around God's Law as a unified and will-determining center.[30]

With the founding of Agudat Israel, the transcendent has become empirical once again. Israel has arisen from "historical anonymity." In religious terms, redemption has been partially, proleptically achieved by the act of restoring the sovereignty of God over Israel through the concrete polity which Agudah represents.

In Rosenheim's conception, the founding and shaping of Agudat Israel has symbolic significance of both historical and cosmic proportions. Politics, a formerly peripheral activity, has become the center. Political action becomes a privileged way of realizing divine will. The actions of the reborn body of Israel in history reflect the destiny of the divine in the world. Agudah becomes the symbolic center of the Jewish lifeworld. Its internal organization, committees, meetings, decisions and rituals "will mark" to use a phrase of Clifford Geertz's, "the center as center and give what goes on there its aura of being not merely important but in some odd fashion connected with the way the world is built."[31]

The way the Agudah was "built" was to symbolize how God rules over Israel, given the pluriform, diaspora reality of the Jews. The constitution of the movement is an amalgam of modern democratic institutions and ancient hierarchical structures. Any Jew who "recognizes the binding nature of the Torah for himself and the Jewish people" could join.[32] The primary structures were independent local associations. These were unified on the national level in the various European states. Each national group had a governing board, selected democratically from the local associations and a rabbinical council also chosen from the membership. The national groups sent delegates to a convention (*Kenessiah Gedolah* or "great assembly") scheduled to meet every five years. The Kenessiah Gedolah, in turn, elected one hundred of its members into a Central Committee, which—in its various subcommittees—ran Agudat Israel until the next round of elections. Atop the whole structure was the Council of Torah Sages (*Moetzet G'dolei ha-Torah*). The practical function of the Council was to determine whether proposed political courses of action accorded with or violated the Torah. The Council thus had veto power over any policy the Central Committee might advocate. Symbolically, the Council linked Agudat Israel with the ancient Sanhedrin. Rosenheim was explicit about this: Agudat Israel, under the guidance of its sages, was to function for world Jewry as the Sanhedrin did for the Jewish polity of antiquity. Again, we see the seamless welding—from the point of view of our historical subject—of ancient norms and practices with modern institutions and means. Do these ancient ideals and customs simply endure or are they consciously reclaimed and deliberately manipulated? Is tradition naturally reenacted or is it, in Eric Hobsbawm's phrase, "invented" by modern movements, such as Agudah, searching for popular legitimacy?[33] Put abstractly, how much and what kind of continuity is required to speak of tradition in general and of the Jewish political tradition in particular? I have already suggested that tradition lives, at least in part, on the belief of the traditionalist that he or she stands within a certain stream of development. But certainly, to claim that tradition "x" endures over time, there must also be more objective evidence of continuity. The traditions of skill practiced by craftsmen, for example, are manifest in the stylistic continuity of the objects they produce. If they merely believe that they are carrying on the practices of earlier artisans, but their work gives no evidence of it, we should doubt that the tradition really remains in force. Similarly, we want to find more objective evidence of continuity of practices, institutions, and relationships such that we can claim that a Jewish political tradition endures. It is my view that continuities exist both objectively and subjectively: that Agudah *both* envisioned itself within a stream of tradition *and* created structures which were adaptations of inherited institutions received from a long past. I hope to demonstrate therefore in the pages that follow that Agudat Israel is an instance of the way the Jewish tradition has typically expressed the continuum of political-religious experience.

Until recently, modern social science overlooked or marginalized the category of tradition out of deep bias. Studies of modernization often had a normative agenda. Modernization acquired a teleological, evolutionary value. Tradition became an impediment which modernizing societies needed to overcome. The reality, of course, was a great deal more complex. Tradition was never a monolith of consensus or uniformity, was never static, and was never opposed by an alleged monolith called "modernity." S. N. Eisenstadt, for example, demonstrated the continuity of tradition over and despite the caesura of modernity, arguing that patterns of center-periphery relationship, status and symbolic legitimation within modern societies continue to evince premodern antecedents.[34] Other studies, shorn of modernist bias, were able to project onto "traditional societies" much of the differentiation, flexibility, and contestation over the meaning of central symbols that modern societies are known to have.[35] These studies set the tone for this investigation.

In the next chapter, I explore in greater conceptual detail the idea of the Jewish political tradition. I look at arguments for and against the postulation of such an ongoing tradition and seek to develop a workable version of the concept adequate to the study of Agudah.

In the second chapter, I explore the characteristics of the Jewish sacred polity as an ideal type. The device of ideal types is introduced in order to describe the model of polity which Agudah leaders thought of as normative. Against their model of what a normative Jewish community was, we may see how

Frankfurt Orthodox Jews created and evaluated their own polity. Using Samson Raphael Hirsch's writings on community, we try to understand the polity's self-representation. What were its political ideals? How did this ideal-typical vision inform the Agudah movement? Furthermore, how accurate was this envisioned or invented relationship of polity and past? What was the relationship of this vision to Jewish political history and tradition? In particular, did the idea of a "sacred polity" significantly underestimate the "profane" elements of Jewish communal life present in all phases of Jewish history? My argument is that it did underestimate those "profane" elements. In particular, traditional Jewish political action was always relatively rational, that is, based on calculations of advantage. A tension between rational action and the dictates of traditional ethical imperatives characterizes the tradition from early times. For Agudah, this traditional tension continues in, for example, early conflicts between laymen and rabbinate about the scope of Jewish law (*halakha*) in political decision making.

The third chapter is largely historical. I relate the founding of Agudah, focusing on the work of Isaac Itzik Halevy and Jacob Rosenheim. I explore the earliest ideological positions and seek to determine the religious and political implications of each. I am particularly interested in how they sought consensus in the face of their very real internal differences. How did they reconcile the ideal and the real, that is, the holiness and cosmic significance of their movement with the very mundane demands of political compromise and organizing?

The Conclusion reflects on the political-religious nexus in modernity, based on the early history of Agudat Israel.

Chapter 1

INTERPRETING THE SACRED POLITY: THE CONCEPT OF THE JEWISH POLITICAL TRADITION

POLITICS AND RELIGIOUS EXPERIENCE

The writings of the German founders of Agudah invite an approach that is attentive to religious consciousness and to how religious consciousness externalizes itself in social and political life. The Agudists might have developed an organization that was explicitly secular, like the B'nai B'rith or the Central Verein, but they did not. Their's was a curious blend of utopianism and realism. Thus Jacob Rosenheim, in his plenary address at the founding Kattowitz Conference, stated:

> It is not a society (*Verein*) alongside other societies that we wish to found; not a merely pragmatic association (*Zweckverband*), whose meaning exhausts itself in the realization of some practical, individual purposes. What

presents itself to us as our highest goal is rather the reanimation of an archetypal Jewish possession: the traditional concept of *Klal Yisrael*—the entirety of Israel's body, filled and borne by its Torah, its organizing soul—which we will realize through our Agudat Israel in the midst of the world of culture, through those technical means which culture now makes available to us.[1]

The German Agudists clothed their movement with a mantle of religious meaning and legitimacy. We have already suggested that a strictly task-oriented, pragmatic view of their endeavor did not suffice for them because of their religious quest for redemption. But how did the Agudists reconcile something as profound as a quest for redemption with the workaday world of political education, lobbying, and organizing? How did the founders of Agudah conceive the relationship between their Jewish faith and their political action? Was the relationship one of harmony or one of tension?

Contemporary fundamentalist movements, in the United States and elsewhere (including Jewish groups such as Gush Emunim in Israel, which are arguably "fundamentalist") seem to have no problem identifying particular policies with God's will. But such simplistic equations are far from the spirit of the early Agudah. The German Agudists were fully aware of the tension between a political course of action, which always entails moral ambiguity, and a clear commandment of the Torah. In an effort to guard the holiness of the organization against the corrosive implications of overt partisan activity, Agudah's mission statement from Kattowitz excludes the organization from "every political tendency." But this was a rule made to be broken. Thus, a constant problem of the early Agudah was how, in fact, to define politics. How is politics related to the mitzvot? To ethics? Where does politics begin and Torah-oriented action end? Rosenheim's, Breuer's, Halevi's, and others' writings are not straightforward attempts at a synthesis of religion and politics. On the contrary, they are attempts to define and relate two poorly defined and mutable concepts or, alternatively, to reconcile the tension between two poles of a continuum.

Correlating politics and religion is a recurrent problem even in the most integral of traditional societies. Politics requires novel action based on a rational appraisal of a situation. Political agents are required to take account of the probable consequences of different courses of conduct, to weigh possible risks against benefits. This open-ended, calculative rationality is in tension with religious thought and action. Religious thought and action are typically oriented toward ideal ethical values. Absolute ends and duties, given in revelation by a prophet, for example, require faith and submission. They resist being treated as merely possible or desirable ends and hypothetical duties. They are not justified by their consequences, but by their inherent rightness. Furthermore, religious action is typically oriented toward reenacting paradigmatic sacred practices, derived from a divine source *in illo tempore*. This conflicts with the essential novelty of political action. While religious conduct is typically mimetic, political action is often strategic. It does not aim to reenact primordial patterns, but to bring new states of affairs into being.

This tension is moderated to a significant degree in Judaism where law, with its emphatically this-worldly orientation, mediates between absolute, religious ends and ordinary, fallible human activity. Law, which lives and developes by responding to continual change allows for the pursuit of absolute ends in a realistic fashion. It introduces a degree of ends/means rationality into Jewish religious consciousness. But law brings its own problems as well. There is still the tendency to assimilate the decision making required by the present to the hallowed template of the past. Law, by its nature, must analogize the novel to the precedential. Thus a legal orientation, as we will see, imposes its own constraints on the creativity of political action.

So how can political action claim its sanction in a sacred law without hypocrisy? How can the custodians of the sacred and the custodians of public affairs co-exist? How has Jewish society throughout the ages dealt with the inherent tension between the two ideal-typical tendencies of politics and religion? Once we get a clearer view of how the tradition has dealt with this problem, we can judge whether the Agudist approach exemplifies previous Jewish solutions to the problem. If so, then we can point to a dimension of objective continuity between modernity and the political tradition of the Jewish past.

To understand how the Agudist correlation of politics and religion accords with prior models in Judaism, we need to survey a number of historical cases. But we also need to develop an ideal type of Jewish polity and compare the polity of Agudat Israel with it. An ideal type represents the normative ideals of a group, crystalizing their practices and underlying values in a pure, abstract way. As such, it represents what the thought and action of members of the group would look like if they were rationally consistent with the group's own values.[2] Ideal types are meant to provide an empathetic bridge between researcher and subject. They allow us access to the way in which the subject endows human affairs with significance.

Such a comparison would make eminent sense to the Agudists themselves. As traditionalists, German Orthodox Jews were acutely concerned with the correspondence of their beliefs and practices with those of the hallowed past, as they understood it. That is, they operated with their own ideal typical image of the Jewish polity. Rosenheim writes as if the meetings of Agudah committees cast the shadow of the ancient Sanhedrin. To ask how the actors understood and planned their action in light of their beliefs about prior Jewish political tradition, we shall need to specify what they believed about Jewish political organization and action.

Representing the ideal type of the Jewish polity is the business of scholars of the Jewish political tradition. This relatively new field is beset by its own methodological problems to which we shall next turn. We shall discuss the concept at a high level of abstraction, in terms of the different methodological approaches currently used. After clarifying these approaches—including the one used in what follows—we will develop, in the next chapter, an account of what Frankfurt Orthodoxy understood the ideal type of the Jewish polity to be.

APPROACHES TO THE JEWISH POLITICAL TRADITION

In recent years, a growing group of scholars has argued that there is a Jewish political tradition. Such a tradition, they claim, is constituted by an ongoing experience of political institutions internal to the Jewish community, by practical reasoning about such institutions and their relationship to external political structures, and by an incipient, if rather underdeveloped, theoretical analysis of this experiential base. Such thinking is novel. It did not appear plausible to Salo Baron several generations ago, for example, that his work on the ancient and medieval Jewish community concerned Jewish politics. He explicitly denies this.[3]

Yet how could one doubt the existence of such a tradition? Undeniably, Jews have had a long and diverse experience of self-government and have produced a variety of institutional arrangements to structure their communal life. One must also admit that the Jews have engaged in practical reasoning—what Leo Strauss called "political thought"—about the grounds of such arrangements as well as why and how they function. One even finds, in the works of Maimonides and Abravanel, although in few other places, meta-level theoretical reflections on political matters, which Strauss called "political philosophy."[4] While such reflections are structured around presuppositions about the nature of politics derived from non-Jewish sources such as Plato, Jewish adaptations are not lacking.[5] Given all of these phenomena should they not be grouped under the rubric "the Jewish political tradition?"

Part of the problem—the part which troubled Baron—is what we mean by "political." As we have seen, politics, especially in conjunction with religion, is a rather plastic concept. In Baron's context, politics had to do with the behavior of nation-states, conceived in nineteenth century terms as sovereign units monopolizing all law and power over their territory. If that is what politics means, then Jews have not had much political experience since the demise of their ancient commonwealth.

The equation of the political with conditions of fully sovereign statehood is not made only by Jewish modernists. A traditional rabbinic scholar, such as Israel Schepansky in his encyclopedic compendium of Jewish communal legislation, explicitly argues against secular historians such as Simon Dubnow that Jewish self-governance in the medieval *kehillah* cannot be confused with politics. Dubnow claimed that the political tradition of kingship metamorphized into various forms, including the civil administration of the *kehillah*. The *kehillah* was a kingdom in miniature. Schepansky utterly rejects this claim as a piece of secular, Haskalah optimism. He claims that Jews who were committed to Torah denied themselves such illusions because they knew they were in exile and they knew that politics, in the full sense, belongs only to the messianic age.[6] Yet Schepansky's dogmatic judgment does not accord with the medieval sources he himself cites, many of which derive the authority of public institutions from the Deuteronomic laws of kingship. He, no less than the modernist Baron or Dubnow, is influenced by a modern European conception of politics based on the philosophical idea of a reified State.

The definition of politics has, however, shifted. What allows us to talk today about a Jewish polity and not merely about a Jewish community is a broader definition of politics. Thus, Eli Lederhendler writes,

> political analysis has come to include—in addition to the state and international relations—a host of other players (interest groups, lobbies, elites and other social classes, ethnic groups, mobilized diasporas, etc.), structures (parties, bureaucracies, organizations, legislatures, churches, local government, tribes, even the family), and problems ("ethnopolitics," nationalism, colonialism, revolution, leadership, political "mobilization" or participation, labor relations, "modernization," "development," "civil religion," ideology, political myths, political culture and political socialization, public opinion and voter behavior, "core" vs. "periphery").[7]

This broadening of the concept of politics has come about for various reasons: postwar awareness of the destructiveness of nationalism; post-colonial awareness of persisting traditional societies and tribal peoples who exist without a state; as well as an appreciation of the American relativization of state sovereignty. The American tradition of derived public authority versus European philosophical habits of reifying the State focuses attention on all of those public processes which generate authoritative institutions.[8] This broadened conceptual framework can easily take the political experience of diaspora Jews into account.

Changes in the agenda of Jewish studies, as Lederhendler points out, have also facilitated a conceptual shift.[9] The turn toward social history, spurred by historians such as Baron himself, has decisively overturned the paradigm of nineteenth century *Wissenschaft des Judentums*, which saw the Jews as a spiritual nation that transcends politics. In addition, historians have begun to question the influence of the Holocaust—the nadir of Jewish powerlessness—and the founding of the State of Israel—the "Jewish return to history"—on historiography. Should the millenial Jewish political experience be conceptualized on the basis of generalization from the Holocaust experience of complete powerlessness and the pre–1948 fact of statelessness? The formulation, "Jewish politics if and only if Jewish (post–1948) sovereignty," appears to be quite unhistorical. If Jews had not possessed political skills and sagacity, Ismar Schorsch asked, how could they have survived? Indeed, at the source of this marginalization of the political dimension of Jewish life, Daniel J. Elazar suggests, stands the apologetic motive of facilitating assimilation into the modernizing nation states of the Emancipation era. Jews rejected or transformed their own tradition of political self-definition in order to become citizens of their host countries. With the demise of the medieval *kehillah*, came the decline of politically oriented conceptions of Judaism. A sociologist of knowledge might turn to Spinoza and then Mendelssohn for appropriate intellectual images of a late medieval/early modern, post-political Judaism.[10]

On the face of it then, the attribution of a political tradition to the Jews or Judaism should not, given the various paradigm shifts, be problematic. Yet problems do arise on at least two levels. The first is that of the part and the whole. Does Judaism *have* a political tradition, as we might claim it has a musical tradition, or *is* Judaism a political tradition? That is, is politics essential to Judaism? Is the project of recovering the putative Jewish political tradition analogous to recovering, for example, Judaism's teachings about the environment or is the category conceptually fundamental? Conceptualization aside, do Jews need to *live* in a Jewish polity, diaspora, or Israeli, to practice Judaism in any meaningful or recognizable sense or can a meta-political, spiritualized Judaism, such as Franz Rosenzweig's, be normative? Rosenheim and other Frankfurt separatist Jews clearly believed that the political organization of the Jews was necessary to the full realization of Judaism.

The problem of part and whole ineluctably shifts the concept of the Jewish political tradition from a strictly descriptive one to a quasi-theological, prescriptive one. While this may be an unwise or illegitimate move in social science, it nonetheless animates, as we shall see, some of the pertinent studies. It cannot be avoided. Daniel Elazar ascribes a significant normative dimension to the Jewish political tradition. David Biale, by contrast, treats the tradition in a largely descriptive fashion. For Elazar, the tradition contains normative principles which we disregard at our peril. For Biale, the tradition simply provides historical data about previous Jewish successes and failures from which we might, at an appropriate level of generalization, learn.

Another level of problematic, not entirely distinct from the first, is the question of continuity. Is this an unbroken, essentialistic tradition of determinant intellectual and structural content such that we can specify that elements x and y (e.g., covenant and consent) endure over time? Or does it suffice that tradition designate an open-ended category in which all sorts of political phenomena can fit (e.g., theocracy, monarchy, democracy)? Logically speaking, what are the existence conditions for predicating "tradition?" How much continuity is logically required in order to posit a tradition? How we resolve this will depend on our theory of tradition as such.

What we might call the maximalist tendency is repre-sented by Daniel Elazar.[11] He interprets the social arrange-ments and many of the chief documents of Judaism as essen-tially political phenomena and ascribes a high level of continuity to Jewish political structures. Elazar believes that while each epoch of Jewish history evolves its own terminol-ogy for Jewish political institutions, these institutions and the vocabulary which represents them evince a continuous tradi-tion, whose origins lie in biblical Israel. In the Bible, for exam-ple, a chief political designation for the community is *edah*. In the middle ages, the appropriate term is *kehillah*. In the mod-ern diaspora, "voluntary community" is an appropriate desig-nation. In every case however, an underlying structure—the political community as res publica rather than as the private preserve of a single sovereign—is in force. The underlying structure is expressive of the constitutive values of Judaism. Jewish political tradition is an ongoing dialogue about those values within the relative fixity of the framework of the Torah/constitution. Thus in Elazar's view, the tradition con-sists of both a conceptual framework, rooted in the ideas and values of the Bible, and a sequence of institutions, comprising the structural basis of the tradition.

Before exploring the maximalist view further, we might mention some of the scholarship of the previous generation which anticipates this position. At least insofar as the maxi-malist view posits a highly political quality for the whole of Judaism, it is probably indebted to the thought of Leo Strauss. Strauss did much to stimulate reflection on the relationship of Judaism to political philosophy and science. In his work on Maimonides, Strauss effectively implied that Judaism not only has a political tradition, but *is* a political tradition. Strauss believed Maimonides to hold that "the function of the Torah is emphatically political."[12] Much of the Torah, in Strauss's read-ing of Maimonides, is devoted to the "governance of the city." Thus Strauss began to correct the prevalent apolitical concep-tualization of Judaism, albeit in a limited application. He raised the suspicion that if Judaism is essentially political, then fully apolitical interpretations of Jewish existence, such as that of Franz Rosenzweig, need to be heavily qualified.[13]

The insight into the political nature of Judaism opens up innumerable, previously foreclosed, implications. In Strauss's case, his appreciation of the political character of Judaism, led him to understand much of medieval Jewish thought as an application of Platonic political philosophy. The political turn led Strauss to argue for the superiority of medieval Jewish thought vis a vis the modernist bias toward apolitical existentialism and personalism.[14]

Strauss was not alone in this turn toward the political. His fellow German Jewish emigre, the eminent historian Yitzhak Baer, argued for a sustained and substantive Jewish political tradition reaching back to the Bible and extending into the medieval *kehillah*. The tradition has both distinctive institutional structures and normative values. Baer came to the conclusion that, since Judaism is inescapably political, basic Jewish oral law needs to be understood as constitutional in character.[15] Indeed, Louis Finkelstein anticipated Baer in this conclusion as early as 1924.[16]

This twentieth century scholarly openness to rehabilitating the political dimension of historical and contemporary Judaism no doubt owes something to the success of Zionism, modern Jewry's most successful political project. This is not, however, without irony. For Zionism saw itself as a break with the (allegedly apolitical) Jewish past. The diaspora was to be negated as an abnormal phase of abject powerlessness. Accordingly, some Zionist historiography has tended to negate the value, or to even deny the presence of political tradition in the Jewish past. Nonetheless, the cumulative effect of Jewish national rebirth and the reassertion of state sovereignty exceeds Zionism's own ideological logic.

To get a clearer view of what Elazar's "maximalism" affirms we can contrast it with an "old-line" Zionist-statist view. At the other extreme, Gerson Weiler articulates a traditional Zionist view which, following Spinoza, reads political concerns out of Judaism altogether. (Since he sees politics and Judaism as wholly mutually exclusive, one hesitates to call him a "minimalist." That designation will be apt for others, however.) For Weiler, Jewish history, post–1948, is radically distinct from what preceded it. With statehood, the Jews have returned to politics and history. Their nationhood has at last found a fit context, albeit a context which is problematically related to Judaism. Zionism is incompatible, for the most part, with Judaism insofar as the latter has, allegedly, a weak political tradition.

All of these issues were adumbrated in Spinoza. In the *Theologico-Political Treatise*, Spinoza argued that the Jews were indeed a political people and that their law was the law of a state.[17] While suited to them and designed for their earthly, "emphatically political" benefit, it was, however, flawed. The Hebrew commonwealth divided power against itself. Spinoza sees Israelite history as a record of political decline. The free people who stood at Sinai and covenanted directly with God soon lost their democratic sovereignty by accepting the rule of priests and kings. This loss of primal equality led to resentment and, eventually, sedition. The Torah-constitution, by tolerating, indeed, enshrining inequalities of status spurred the internal weakening of the state.[18] While Israelite government went from relatively bad to wholly bad over the course of its history, the seeds of destruction were sown at the very beginning with the idea (and reality) of theocracy, for God gave the people the laws that made political life unstable from the start.

Ever since the collapse of the Israelite state a once political people has been living a ghostly, anachronistic existence. The law, no longer rooted in the political life of a state, endures. The people obey what remains of their law, but its artificiality—its apolitical character—dooms the people to a marginal, unreal existence. Spinoza holds out the hope that the people may yet return to their land and reconstitute themselves as a political nation but to do so, they would have to abandon their Judaism, which, in the present, emasculates them.[19] Thus, on Spinoza's account, Jews and Judaism fail to be political in two ways. First, the Jews do not actually have a state. Second, Judaism is a post-political artifact, which, by "emasculating" the Jews, prevents them from regaining a state. Regaining a state would involve the repudiation of their theocratic tradition. Judaism, it would seem, offers no resources for that reclamation. Indeed, it is the principal barrier to it.

Basing himself on Spinoza's position, Gershon Weiler argues that Judaism is an antipolitical religion and that the Jews were, until recently, a post-political people.[20] Weiler believes that the Jews were once a "normal" political nation ruled by kings. With the loss of sovereignty over their land, the Jews became less a nation than a "holy community," governed by a code of antipolitics, the halakha. The correct term to describe this community and its law is "theocracy." Theocracy was, in fact, coined by Josephus who affirmed this essentially post-political mode of existence out of both personal exigency and religious conviction.

Weiler is more radical than Spinoza, however. Spinoza at least saw the Torah, however flawed, as the constitution of a state. The survival of the Torah after the fall of the state is an incongruity, but at least at one point the Torah was (more or less) politically fit. Weiler does not postulate a time when the Torah was compatible with political existence. The political, he assumes, is inherently anti-transcendental. Politics cannot concern divine-human relations. It is entirely a matter of the prudential; of *raison d'etat*.[21] Torah, as developed by the rabbis, is a deliberate design for rendering Jewish existence post- and antipolitical. Thus Weiler not only offers a fundamental critique of rabbinic Judaism, but he characterizes the political philosophical expressions of that Judaism, Maimonides and Abravanel, as apologies for an halachic theocracy that is post-political by design.[22]

For Weiler, the tension between politics and religion is so overwhelming that it cannot in any way be resolved. Jews have not, since the destruction of their state, been involved in any activity properly called politics, nor could they value such an activity. This conclusion follows not only from his statist premises, but also from his basic understanding of religion as a fundamentally other-worldly and absolute ethos. Yet this conclusion clearly does damage to both the phenomenology of Judaism and to the actualities of Jewish history. At this point, Daniel Elazar's conception of a politically engaged Judaism and Jewish people shows its advantages.

Elazar, in contrast to Weiler, holds that the State of Israel, rather than constituting an absolute break with the Jewish past, is located to a certain extent within the stream of a Jewish political tradition which has helped to produce it. Elazar denies that the Jewish people has fundamentally changed its mode of existence.[23] While Weiler sees a great divide between an Israelite/Judean nation-state and a postexilic, theocratic holy community, Elazar sees a continuum. In his view, a basic pattern persists. Covenant is the essential, ongoing structural element of Jewish political existence. Indeed, covenant is the constitutive mode of Israel's being. Israel's covenant with God creates and recreates a unique society which realizes itself in different forms of political organization, all of which are federative (that is, covenantal) in nature. In federative forms of organization, power is diffused across competing institutional centers. Since ultimate power is God's alone, human institutions are deabsolutized and conditional. Descriptively, federative or covenantal organization is the typical form of Jewish polity. Normatively, it is the optimal form of Jewish political order. Elazar therefore sees any version of statism, inspired by modern European political thought, as alien to and incompatible with the Jewish political tradition.

Elazar writes a constitutional history of the Jews. In every epoch, the Jews exercise power over themselves whether in the context of an independent state, an autonomous community, or a voluntary association. That power is invariably dispersed in competing offices: priests, kings, and prophets in one era, rabbis and exilarchs in another. These centers of power, using a mishnaic term, are designated *ketarim* (crowns). At every point, the people constitute themselves covenantally before God and rally around constitutions which ratify the covenantal act. Thus, the Mosaic Torah, the Mishna, the Shulhan Arukh are styled as constitutional instruments which order the institutional arrangements and political-cultural values of their epochs. The premise of federative or covenantal self-organization allows Elazar to minimize the political import of catastrophes such as the loss of Judean independence in the sixth century B.C.E. Furthermore, the assertion of an essentialistic pattern beneath phenomenalistic changes of regime allows him to find a singular political tradition where others find heterogeneity and discontinuity. His project is to describe and recover that tradition and to provide a theoretical articulation of its particular political values. He suggests that this recovery and formulation is of high importance for the Jewish political future.[24] Just as Weiler accepts the full import of Spinoza's critique, Elazar turns what Spinoza took to be a vice into a virtue. Competing centers of power, which Spinoza thought fatal to political stability, are seen as the key to Jewish political longevity.

David Biale occupies a midpoint between Weiler and Elazar. Biale believes in a coherent Jewish political tradition but does so in a truly minimalist way. Biale rejects Weiler's concept of national independence. The idea of an autonomous, sovereign nation-state is a modern phenomenon which Weiler has anachronistically retrojected onto the biblical past. Politics does not require a "normal" nation-state in the modern sense as its bearer. The people Israel, regardless of the institutional form its national life has taken has always been political, for the Jews have always lived in relation to gentile political structures and forces. Following Ismar Schorsch, Biale asserts that the survival of Jews throughout the centuries represents a canny and effective appraisal of political reality and a communal policy of securing room to maneuver within that reality. For Biale, politics is constituted by group struggle on the stage of history. To the extent that this can always be posited of the Jews, the Jews have always been political.[25]

On the other hand, Biale rejects Elazar's essentialism as metahistorical in formulation and mechanical in application.[26] He sees an ongoing engagement with the realities of power, but not a strong tradition of deliberate covenantal-constitutional organization. The history of internal Jewish institutional arrangements displays complete heterogeneity. Nonetheless, he posits a minimalist version of a framework by discerning an ongoing attempt to ground those arrangements in a formal, even theoretical way at least within premodern rabbinic Judaism.[27] Medieval Jews creatively adapted biblical and talmudic materials to legitimate their own *kehillot*. The Jews are thus political both by design and by default. As do the other scholars, Biale derives contemporary political implications from his analysis. The Jews have fared best politically when they have been prudential and have kept transcendent considerations out of their calculations. Prudence has tended to neutralize messianism. The political has been kept pragmatic. Thus, the volatile messianism of religious fundamentalism or the imprudent over-estimation of Israel's power and sovereignty departs from the main lines of the Jewish political tradition.

For Biale, the Jewish political tradition is "a persistent tradition of political imitation and accomodation, but never of passivity or retreat from politics."[28] This sentence discloses some of the working assumptions which cause him to doubt Elazar's project and incline him toward a weaker characterization of tradition. It is clear that Biale aims to restore an image of the Jews as political agents, actively shaping their own communal destiny throughout their history. It is equally clear that they get little unambiguous moral help from their tradition in the process. The tradition appears as a source and a scene of conflict rather than as a normative orientation. The tradition will tell us, for example, that the parties of accomodation with prevailing power realities have always been opposed by parties aspiring to full sovereignty who incline toward revolt.[29] Biale sees this antagonism as more or less constant in Jewish history. The tradition will not tell us however which party best represents Judaism. That is a normative judgment about which Judaism is silent. Indeed "Judaism" is a reified abstraction, if we refer to something that allegedly transcends its constitutive conflicts. In Elazar's work, by contrast, tradition is cast in a far more normative or prescriptive mold.

By recalling Biale's earlier work, *Gershom Scholem: Kabbalah and Counterhistory*, we get some clues to his historiographic orientation. In the present work, I suggest, Biale has written a "counterhistory" of the Jews as political animals, informed by his understanding of Scholem's orientation.

Counterhistory consists of unearthing and revealing dynamic, historical forces which apologetic historians have repressed or marginalized for the sake of some doctrinaire representation of Jewish history. Scholem's counterhistorical method brought him to oppose the antiquarianism and dogmatism of nineteenth century *Wissenschaft des Judentums*. He rediscovered and emphasized the irrational elements of Judaism, seeing in mysticism an undercurrent of vitality for Judaism as a whole. Counterhistory exposes the mutual interaction of "normative" and subterranean in Judaism. Tradition becomes an arena where conflicting forces struggle, without resolution, for hegemony. Tradition, in Scholem's view, "does not merely consist of conservative preservation, the constant continuation of the spiritual and cultural possessions of a community . . . There are domains of [tradition] that are hidden under the debris of centuries and lie there waiting to be discovered and turned to good use . . . There is such a thing as a treasure hunt within tradition."[30] Tradition is not only dynamic; it is a conjunction of opposites, a field of dynamic conflicts between opposing forces. Scholem's counterhistory is an anarchistic attempt to show the plurality of competing sources of authority in historical Judaism. Scholem shows how the apocalyptic, the demonic, the torrential force of irrationalism are the constant historical companions of the pragmatic, the orthodox, the halakhic. The task of the historian is to display this vibrant and vitalizing "productive conjunction of opposites" as well as to unmask the dogmatic biases of those historians who would resolve Judaism into a single, nondialectical essence.[31]

Like Scholem vis a vis the *Wissenschaft* tradition, Biale also subverts inherited representations of Jewish history, in this case those of an apolitical, passive, theocratic community. Each historian opposes those dogmatic representations which supress the diversity of the historical record in the name of some spiritual or rational essentialism. Each opposes any representation that divorces the Jews from primary, irrational sources of vitality. Just as Scholem wrote counterhistory using the precision tools of the *Wissenschaft* he sought to discredit (all the while eschewing non-*wissenschaftlich* approaches to the irrational such as Martin Buber's) so too Biale claims to work empirically and inductively, eschewing what he takes to be dogmatism in Elazar and Weiler. Indeed, that is why counterhistory is history and not merely uncontrolled imaginative construction. But of course there is no method without presuppositions, and Biale's treatment, deriving from a "counterhistorical" inclination, may cause him to underestimate or overlook the potential continuities in Jewish political history to which Elazar is attuned.

Biale's unwillingness to construct the Jewish political tradition as a normative tradition stems from more than the value-free orientation of the social scientist. It derives, I suggest, from Scholem's anarchist philosophy of Jewish history. (I use the word philosophy with caution as it ascribes a higher level of systematic articulation of principles than is warranted.) Since the tradition is a tradition of conflicting forces, there is no sure guide to which force is normative. Anarchism is not a denial of any source of authority, as is nihilism, but a sober recognition of a plurality of authorities (without the doctrinaire faith that they are all of equal worth, i.e., pluralism).[32] Although Biale assures us that this anarchism is not relativism, exactly how this position is saved from relativism is unclear.[33]

The argument between Daniel Elazar and David Biale derives in no small measure from the differing assumptions behind their interpretative practices: Biale's hermeneutic is consistently suspicious, Elazar's aims toward empathy. Elazar has a willingness to use sources normatively, while Biale has a predominating commitment to empirical description, coupled with an anarchistic suspicion of ascribing authority to texts. Elazar believes in continuities, however dynamic, at the levels of both institutional content and intellectual framework, while Biale has a tentative assumption of continuity at the level of framework and an agnosticism toward continuity at the level of contents. There is little point in trying to reconcile these positions. They ought to be judged by how productive they are of questions which yield new insight into the historical material. But insofar as Elazar's approach is better suited to a study of Agudat Israel, I do wish to argue, however, two specific points against Biale to secure a position close to Elazar's (without, however, committing myself to all of Elazar's judgments regarding empirical, historical matters and methodological issues such as periodization).

Elazar's view seems preferable to me for two reasons. First, it allows for diversity and conflict within living tradition without overstating their role and understating the possibility of continuity. Second, Elazar's view seems more adequate from a phenomenological point of view. That is, to return to our initial point, its openness to normative issues, to discerning a normative voice within Jewish tradition, accords better with the experience of the producers of and participants in the Jewish cultural drama than does a more or less strict, inductive-empirical approach.

THE STUDY OF TRADITION

Biale's minimalist understanding of tradition in the face of the disruptive heterogeneity of counterhistory is overly skeptical toward the role of tradition in the maintenance of society. There is no reason to doubt as a working hypothesis that various political values and preferences for institutional design have continued across Jewish history. It is possible to say that these values have been contested or that the institutions they produce have been quite variegated and still assert an underlying, substantive continuity. It is also possible to make this claim on the basis of induction and the empirical observation of social life rather than on the basis of dogmatism.

What argues in favor of the substantive continuity of tradition, in this case political tradition, over discontinuity is the sheer fact of the survival of the Jewish people in an organized, societal fashion. For any society to survive, that is, for

members of a group at one point in history to believe themselves to be members of the same group as their ancestors
requires that a trans-generational consensus exist.[34] Without
some ongoing agreements, society, or at least parts of society,
destructures into a horde. The living must accept the beliefs
and institutions presented to them by the dead, even while
changing or arguing over them. Thus, societies endure because
they are constantly reenacted. Patterns of assertions and
actions, inherited from the past, are realized over and again in
the present.

Substantive traditions—beliefs, practices, rules, texts,
objects—are transmitted from generation to generation. The
chief transmissive channels for this reenactment are family,
Church (in Troeltsch's sense) and educational system. These
channels present the beliefs and practices of the past for the
adoption and adaptation of the present. It is unthinkable, even
in the most "progressive" of contemporary schools or
churches to avoid a continual absorption of the past. A revolutionary regime may rewrite history, but it cannot withhold
the teaching of its own history to its young if it hopes to survive. No society can ensure its future without incessant contemplation and reenactment of its past. The reenactment of
what is remembered from the past; of what the present members of society believe the past members expect from them
ensures a thread of continuity. Indeed, the belief that there *is* a
thread of continuity is a necessary but not sufficient condition
for the endurance of society. This thread of memory and
expectation is what Biale's view appears to deny and Elazar's
confirms.

To say that the members of present society act according
to how they are expected to act, with the pattern of expectations having been shaped by past generations is to introduce a
strongly normative element into the account of how tradition
functions. Societies persist due to their traditions. Traditions
persist because their adherents find them right and good or, at
least, convenient and efficacious. When traditions, rules of
etiquette, for example, cease to solve the social problems they
were created to expedite, they wither and are rejected or

replaced. But until the point when specific traditions become dysfunctional—often because of their long-ripening conflict with other traditions—they enjoy the loyalty and approval, if only critical approval, of their adherents.

No society can exist without tradition, but some societies, especially premodern ones, cultivate and value their traditions more than other societies. Whereas modern men and women resent the grip of the past as a "metaphysical encumberance" on their freedom, so-called traditional societies derive their bearings from the inheritance of their past, shunning the chaos that would ensue in an historical vacuum. They find their traditions not only useful, but morally necessary.

This normative dimension of tradition is pervasive in the Jewish case. The Torah tends toward leaving no area of life void of possible connection with the sacred. Therefore, Jewish traditions, grounded in the earliest ages of Jewish civilization, seek to comprehend the whole of life and bring it into a numinous sphere. There is no sphere where tradition might not, in principle, pertain.[35] Living under a regime of tradition, seeking to construct both personal and social life against the hallowed templates of the past, the premodern Jew innovated new forms, but justified them in terms of affinities with elements from the stock of tradition. Innovation could not be justified in the name of innovation, but only in the name of the past and the authority it conveyed on the innovators of the present. Yet this very pastness should not be viewed as a mere pretext. It should be viewed as the substantive context in which innovation, which is the modification of tradition, occured.

Add to this the nonterritorial, nonsovereign nature of diaspora Jewish life and we see that the sacralized, constitutive traditions of Judaism had a very high salience as the surest means of social survival. The Jewish present was a reenactment of patterns from the stock of traditions tendered by the past. This is not to say that those traditions were static, uncontested, or one-dimensional. Nor is it to say that those traditions were not constantly enriched, influenced and coerced by, as well as creatively adapted to, the beliefs, practices and expectations of non-Jewish society. It is however to say that to even speak of a tradition, we must assume a level of substantive content; a *something* to be transferred and transformed.

When Biale asserts that the Jewish political tradition consists of no more than "persistent imitation and accomodation" he is caught in self-contradiction. What is traditional here? Imitation is a practice that can occur in a perpetual present. Who needs to remember anything in order to imitate what one sees around one? Creatures such as minah birds, whose lives are governed by instinct not tradition, can imitate. Perhaps a "tradition of imitation" means remembering how to imitate and believing that the practice of imitation has value. But when we speak of tradition in this sense, we are already positing a substantive continuity of practice and value, which Biale is loath to do. How can there be recurrent patterns of action, such as parties of accomodation and parties of resistance, unless these patterns of action are remembered? If there is a thread of memory, how can one claim that there is no continuity? Memory by definition implies the diachronic persistence of that which is remembered.

Of course, memory is an active force rather than a passive depository. Memory selects and constructs a usable past. Much of the past is lost, day by day, and what is remembered remains labile. To be sure, not all of the assertions and actions of the past are remembered by actors in the present. But that which does enter into the memory of a group forms an "objective deposit" of tradition which is carried forward as a stock of possibilities and expectations. The members of a tradition-affirming society locate their collective intellectual project within the horizon of tradition. They share a conceptual and moral universe constituted within a substantive traditional context. "To survive and flourish," Alisdaire MacIntyre asserts, "a tradition requires embodiment in the life of institutionalized communities which identify their history with its history. To belong to a tradition is to be engaged in an essentially communal form of rational existence in which persons so engaged offer commentary upon the achievements of their predecessors and upon the limitations of those achievements, commentary which is then subjected to the objections, elaborations, and amendations of others at work in the same tradition."[36]

The political experience of biblical and post-biblical Israel constitutes a stock of normative and historical traditions for the Jewish people. The Jewish political tradition may be formally described as the reabsorption, reenactment and adaptation of those fundamental concepts, values, and norms under the endlessly changing conditions of history. Elazar's model, which does not entirely free itself from Biale's charge of being mechanical, directs us toward discerning the continuity of political ideals as well as political practices. Indeed, if we say that Elazar's model presents an ideal typical pattern of Jewish political thought and action it will have the additional advantage of giving us a key to the normative mentality of the traditional Jew engaged in the practice of communal self-government.

When Biale writes that the doctrine of divine chosenness is a political myth to justify the conquest of Canaan and impose a "myth of unity" on a "fragile political alliance between highly fragmented tribes," he claims something which may or may not be true with regard to the social function of a religious belief.[37] What is lacking in this assertion, however, is the retention of a dimension of the meaning of the belief for its adherents. We prefer to follow Max Weber's approach which sought to determine both the dimension of a belief's significance for the believer, and the social function of the belief. (Weber rejected the view that religious beliefs are strictly or simply caused by political or economic circumstances in favor of the view that there is an "elective affinity" between beliefs and the historical circumstances under which they thrive.) Were Biale to have made this distinction, he would not sound like such a reductionist. Furthermore, Biale's view fails on its own terms. If chosenness is only an idea which provided group cohesion and political legitimation at a certain point in Israelite history, why its continual historical salience? Why didn't it metamorphose into other sorts of belief once the historical circumstances which engendered it changed? The fact that the doctrine of chosenness, despite its many elaborations in the course of the history of Judaism, remains rooted in its biblical contours indicates the status of an ongoing, substantive, intellectual tradition.

One can make a hard-headed historical case for the political usefulness of chosenness, as Biale has done, without reducing chosenness to nothing but a legitimating device. What is missing is the attempt to understand how the historical subjects who thought themselves chosen ordered their lives in light of their belief. Also missing is a sense of the objectivity of the belief: the way that it enters the stock of Jewish traditions and continues to exert a pull on Jewish self-definition throughout the centuries. Functionalism obscures the workings of tradition as an objective force in human affairs.

Elazar's view, by contrast, upholds both the objective and the normative dimensions of tradition. It calls our attention to the way Jews ordered their lives, and defined themselves and their situations, in light of the reality of their traditions. It allows us to be empirical, while freeing us from having to sound cynical, as if all religious discourse masked nothing more than power relations and all religious thought was the transcendental illusion of a false consciousness.

Elazar's view enables us to appreciate the fact that, during the centuries when rabbinic Judaism was dominant and the Jews had substantial communal autonomy, Jews conceived of their leaders as deriving their authority from ancient, divinely mandated sources. The rabbis, commenting on Genesis 49:10, "The scepter shall not depart from Judah," assert that "scepter" refers to the political leader of Babylonian Jewry, the Exilarch. The Exilarchs (roshei galuyot sheb'bavel) have communal authority equivalent to King David.[38] After the demise of the exilarchate and its echoes of royal sovereignty, rabbinic decisors devolved royal authority onto a variety of communal leaderships. The thirteenth century halakhist, R. Menachem Meiri, for example, asserted that "in every generation, the leaders of the time—those preeminent in their respective countries—are authorized to impose sanctions and [even] capital punishment," thus equating communal authority with royal power.[39] The duly constituted communal leadership is as the Patriarch or prince vis-a-vis the member of the community. The great Spanish contemporary of Meiri, R. Solomon b. Abraham Adret, affirmed that "just as all of the individual communities are subservient to the Sanhedrin or to the Patriarch, so too every individual is subservient to the community of his own town."[40] In each of these cases, Jewish legal thinkers creatively adapted the precedent of ancient institutions to contemporary conditions.

These rabbinic leaders clearly saw themselves (and the lay officials of their communities) as belonging to a continuous tradition of derived political authority. One can view this "cynically" as a functional legitimating device, an "ideology," but such an interpretation misses the phenomenological fact of the matter, namely that these believers situated their thought and practice within an ongoing, living political tradition. Their belief that they belonged to such a tradition is an important part of their self-consciousness, of their self-definition.

In the next chapter, we will discuss those structural and normative dimensions of the political tradition which the Orthodox Jews of nineteenth century Frankfurt received and then creatively shaped to respond to their own problems. Confronted by the secularization of their political tradition, they tried to restore and reconstitute its institutions and values under the vastly changed conditions brought about by Emancipation.

Chapter 2

THE SACRED POLITY
IN TRANSITION:
MEDIEVAL NORMS AND
MODERN IDEALS

In this chapter, I want to discuss traditional Jewish conceptions of community and polity. We will try to discern some of the ideal-typical elements of the polity. Those dimensions of the polity which endure over time can thus be seen to constitute typical features of the Jewish political tradition. Against this background, I shall focus on the concept of community of Frankfurt Orthodoxy's leading luminary, Samson Raphael Hirsch. What did Hirsch inherit from the Jewish political tradition? How did he appropriate and adapt it? How did his followers, who constituted the primary source and ideological center of the Agudah movement, understand their situation in the late nineteenth and early twentieth centuries in light of the Jewish political tradition and Hirsch's reading of it? What symbolic self-representation did they project? How did they, as traditional Jews, respond to the increasing secularization of Jewish and general society? How did they propose to transform community into sacred community, indeed, into sacred polity?

The reader of *fin de siecle* Frankfurt Orthodox writings can immediately detect a yearning for what we have called the sacred polity.[1] There is a pervasive sense that the contemporary Jewish community has lost a holy or transcendent dimension and has become a mere social fact—an empirical artifact which no longer opens toward a more sublime horizon of being. The once sacred center has been distorted and deformed by centrifugal forces. The basis of legitimation has shifted from an ontological framework—where the institutions of the polity have authority due to their conformity to a higher law—to a legal or formal one, where public institutions are validated by their compliance with strictly immanent norms. The community may pass some relevant legal or constitutional muster, but it no longer derives its fundamental legitimacy from the transcendent standard of Torah.[2]

Yet to what extent did any historical Jewish community or polity so derive its legitimacy? To what extent was the medieval sacred polity, the *kehillah kedoshah*, fully validated by transcendent norms? To what extent was it an arena that permitted rational ends-means calculation and experimentation? That is, to what extent was the governance of the *kehillah* a *fully* political affair characterized by negotiation, competing interests and claims to power, compromise, and risk taking? To what extent did the *kehillah* view itself, on the other hand, as the enactment of a sacred script, of a heavenly polity on earth wholly determined by Torah law? To what extent were its policy decisions based on Jewish law and considered to be beyond question?[3]

The Orthodox critics of the secularizing nineteenth century Jewish community believed that the Torah provided such a script and that contemporary Jewish political culture represented a massive departure from it. They sought to reappropriate the script and bring the community into conformity with it. If the community is not related to the sacred center, that is, to the Torah as constitution, then it fails to be an object of political obligation. But did the Jewish political tradition in fact provide or require a thorough ontological legitimation for public affairs or did it recognize a sphere of legitimate secularity in which public affairs could be conducted on the basis of rational legislation or practical, efficacious custom? The fact is, of course, that the tradition recognized, from biblical times, a legitimate sphere of secularity in which civil authorities such as the king or the elders or, by tannaitic times, the townsmen (bnei ha-ir) could conduct public affairs according to their own perception of public need and of the public good. How then does this qualify the aspirations of those, like the ideologues of Agudah, who sought to create or, as they saw it, recreate a Torah-validated community? Did they appreciate the extent to which the Torah allowed for a "secular" sphere or did their own need for a redemptive politics overwhelm the Torah's own tradition of tolerating a relatively disenchanted, discretionary domain of action?

The sphere of legitimate secularity that tradition always allowed for can be thought of, in sociological terms, as a domain of *rational action* based on the calculation of appropriate ends and means. For the purposes of the present discussion such a sphere will constitute *politics* in a narrow sense. This fact necessarily qualifies the more theocratic aspirations of some of the communal theoreticians. On the other hand, the ongoing reality of such a politics was in dialectical tension with a countervailing tendency: an impulse to rein in politics and subordinate it to the supervision and legitimization of the custodians of sacred law, that is halakhic scholars. We might call this impulse to subsume politics under an ideally sacral system *administration* based on halakha.[4] This tension runs all the way back to the origins of the Jewish political tradition. It is a tension between a worldview that is open to the irrationality of social life and that seeks to deal with constant change through the application of practical reason and a worldview that would extend a system of sacred law indefinitely from the known into the unknown so that all that is irrational can be rendered lawful.

These tendencies are in conflict. To the extent that administration, based on halakha, replaces politics, based on an autonomous and practical response to social reality, the community appears to its members as a sacred community. A sacred community is one whose public institutions and practices are wholly anchored in transcendent norms. Public policies and practices are believed to reliably reflect the will of God. This belief is undercut by a rational politics. To the extent that politics, implying innovation and the pursuit of rational courses of action, predominates, the community's anchorage in sacred soil is weakened. Politics inclines toward a disenchanted understanding of society, which then invites or requires compensatory re-sacralization. I shall argue that while this immanent dialectic has been present throughout Jewish history, such that it constitutes one of the lines of continuity of the political tradition, early modernity witnessed an intensification of rational, political action. This action came in response to what was perceived as epochal change in the external environment.

Both Samson Raphael Hirsch and his Frankfurt disciples embody this tension. They theorized about "Torah true" political action, thus giving concrete expression to the practical, political traditions of diaspora Jewry. At the same time, they denied that they possessed freedom of political action and believed that they were simply following a sacred script. The attempt to resolve this tension, which resides in the phenomenology of Judaism as such, lends an epochal dimension to the project of the Frankfurt Jews.

The abiding tension between the legitimacy of politics and an utopian consciousness that would resolve politics into sacred administration is fully evident in the thought of Jacob Rosenheim. Rosenheim at once embraces a flexible and rational politics and seeks to subordinate it to halachic norms. He tells us that Agudat Israel, in pursuing its goal of securing the physical and economic security of the Jewish people, needs to preserve the "real-political" flexibility (*realpolitische Schmiegsamkeit*) which is the hallmark of the Jewish political tradition. Jewish leaders have always adapted themselves to prevailing conditions. Whether those conditions have required intercession with medieval monarchs or lobbying modern parliaments, the tradition (and Agudat Israel) is sufficiently pragmatic to work effectively within the political realities.[5] Flexibility, within the ethical guidelines of Judaism, is a proven means.

On the other hand, political decision making must be explicitly tied to halakhic rules and meta-halakhic, ethical norms. Agudat Israel aims at nothing less than raising the Jewish people from a mass of uncoordinated humanity in "historical anonymity" to a nation that realizes God's law, the Torah, in its political life. To do this, the whole nation, represented by Agudat Israel at its symbolic center, must actually be governed by Torah. If a policy cannot be explicitly justified by either a rule or principle of the Torah, as determined by the contemporary sages of the Rabbinical Council, then it cannot be implemented. Rosenheim points, as an especially thorny example, to Agudist policy regarding Palestine. There is widespread disagreement among Orthodox laymen and authorities over what stance to take vis-a-vis colonizing, land purchasing, investment, and so on. If we were to be abandoned to politics alone, however grounded in ethics (as Jewish politics must indeed be), we would still be open to terminal disagreement over these irresolvable issues. Only appeal to the constitutional fundament, the Torah, avails. Agudah's Israel-policy is thus based on the mitzvah of dwelling in the land of Israel.[6] Neither a prophet-like intimation of the world-historical, messianic significance of the Balfour Declaration—Isaac Breuer's view—nor a quietist stance based on a disinclination to be identified with Zionism—the view of many Eastern European leaders—is solid enough to form a basis for policy. The Torah alone decides on the basis of a concrete mitzvah, in principle unchallenged (except by a few authorities under particular conditions).[7]

Rosenheim assumes then that Torah, determined by contemporary rabbinic decisors, both creates the space for a sphere of rational, political activity and frees Jews from having to work solely within such a sphere. Recourse to halakha saves us from both retreat into a private, apolitical pursuit of personal sanctification and from abandonment to public affairs without transcendent purpose. Yet Rosenheim does not exactly resolve the tension between politics and the transcendent in favor of the latter. Despite the legitimating function vouchsafed to the Rabbincal Council, Rosenheim suggests that meta-halakhic, ethical priniciples, growing out of the legal tradition itself, must sometimes take precedence over the rules as such.[8] Rosenheim thus opens a window of opportunity for principled laymen to challenge sages should the need arise. The need did in fact arise, as we shall see below, for Rosenheim to have to challenge the authority of Rabbi Salomon Breuer over the criteria for membership in Agudah.

The tension and inconsistency in Rosenheim's thought, and Agudah's practice, thus continues a tension implicit in and partly constitutive of the Jewish political tradition. This polarization of approaches to public affairs requires both phenomenological and historical investigation. I shall begin with a consideration of the historical issues and then turn to the phenomenological analysis.

THE HISTORICAL SETTING

The Orthodox of the late nineteenth and early twentieth centuries imagined a simpler time, before the onset of modernity, when Ashkenazi Jews lived in integral communities and Torah was the unifying principle and basis of communal life. Writing in September 1911, Rabbi E. Weill, for example, lamented the current historical condition of the Jewish people as both one of exile (*Zerstreuung*), and of an internal exile; of being splintered and torn (*Zersplitterung, Zerrissenheit*) from within.[9] Similarly, Jacob Rosenheim, speaking at one of the early meetings of German Orthodox leaders called to probe the possibilities of a world Orthodox organization stated that:

> If one were to seek a short and precise expression of what is desired, one could say that it has to do with the restora-

tion, in the highest sense, of that Jewish unity, which rests on the basis of the Torah, which still existed at the end of the eighteenth century.[10]

In line with this aspiration, the mission statement of Agudah, adopted at the founding Kattowitz conference in 1912, stated that Agudah must strive for the "organizational unification and inward convergence of the splintered portions of observant Jewry, especially of eastern and western Jewry."[11]

Statements of this order reflect a utopian aspiration for renewal, fueled by *fin de siecle* nostalgia for simpler times. But they also reflect an accurate appraisal of a complex historical situation. In the nineteenth century, Orthodoxy suffered a series of fragmentations. Most importantly, the traditional autonomous Jewish polity, the *kehillah*, a centuries old bastion of Jewish national and corporative existence, was robbed of its political status by the modernizing, centralizing state.[12]

The decline of the *kehillah* came about both due to the incursions of the state and due to the increasing anomie and disaffection of the emerging Jewish middle classes. This *Bildungsbürgertum*, hoping for full integration into German society, rejected Jewish communal autonomy and rabbinic authority as obstacles to full emancipation. They viewed the compulsory, autonomous community as a relic of the Middle Ages which stood in harsh contradiction to the values of a liberal, enlightened age. They promoted a confessionalization of Judaism and a transformation of Jewish community in response to the promise of emancipation. Moses Mendelssohn, in his *Jerusalem*, argued for a Lockean view of religious liberty with a Jewish twist. Insofar as true liberty is inward, that is, Protestant-style "soul liberty," not only must the state not coerce religious obedience, but the coercive powers of the *kehillah* are also immoral. For the Jewish Enlighteners, emancipation meant freedom from both discriminatory civil laws *and* from the traditional Jewish community.[13]

The absolutist state, for its part, endorsed these transformations when they suited its purposes.[14] The modernizing, centralizing state became ever more involved in the internal processes of the Jewish community. The Prussian Jewish regulations (*Judenreglement*) of 1750 abolished rabbinic and lay jurisdiction, thus depriving the *kehillah* of the right to operate its own civil courts according to Talmudic law. Henceforth, the rabbis could only judge strictly "religious" matters.[15] This stipulation appears again in Friedrich Wilhelm III's Edict of Emancipation in 1812, indicating, perhaps, that the Jews were slow to abandon their civil and political institutions. The abolition of these ancient privileges diminished the status of the *kehillah* as a "state within a state," that is, a polity, and initiated its transformation into a religious and ethnic community.

With the decline of communal autonomy, the state deprived the forces of tradition (soon to be called "Orthodoxy" by the party of reform) of the means of coercion, such as the ban, which had earlier silenced dissenters such as Spinoza.[16] As a result, the Orthodox were relegated, by the mid-nineteenth century, to minority status in the state recognized Jewish community (*Gemeinde*). It is important to realize however that, even though the coercive structures of the old *kehillah* disappeared during the nineteenth century and a movement toward the confessionalization of Judaism (i.e., reconstructing Judaism as a religion alone) ensued, the *Gemeinde* itself never fully lost its political dimension. The German states had an interest in retaining the *Gemeinde* as it traditionally provided social services, for example health care and welfare support, for its members. Even after Jews had full access to public services by the middle of the century, the authorities continued to require compulsory membership in the community. It was only Samson Raphael Hirsch's successful campaign for separation from the community in 1876 that terminated the last vestige of communal compulsion.

Thus modernity did not, by any means, end the existence of the Jewish community: it transformed it. As is often the case in the modernization of traditional societies, inherited social structures were not so much rejected as reformulated.[17] The nineteenth century witnessed a renewal of Jewish com-

munal creativity, not a cessation of it. Indeed, the Reform
Jews of Germany, who were most active in promoting a highly
confessionalized, Protestant-oriented conception of Judaism
were at the forefront of this creativity. After they came to
dominate the boards of many of the Jewish communities, they
argued against Orthodox tendencies toward separatism stressing that the unity of the community was paramount.[18] They
also innovated country-wide movements of political mobi-
lization, defense and the rational coordination of services.[19]

Organized, quasi-compulsory community life did not
abate. The Orthodox, however, were no longer in control of
communal politics. They became a party, as it were, having
always to fight for their own interest. Nor were they of a single
perspective on how to construe their interest. Should they
remain within a unified community and fight for halakhically
acceptable facilities for their own use—as the majority of
Orthodox Jews did—or should they separate from the community and pursue their own course, as Samson Raphael
Hirsch and his followers did?

What virtually all Orthodox Jews agreed on in Germany
was that traditional Judaism had to be reinvented as a kind of
confession. Where once there was the unreflective immediacy of a traditional world, the times now called for a consciously formulated, intellectually coherent traditionalism,
which appealed to emotional and rational persuasion in a culture now characterized by religious pluralism.[20] This ideology
did not lack a political dimension. The attempt to persuade
Jews to halakhic obedience was interwoven with the claims of
the rabbinate to exercise its traditional political authority.
The political function of the rabbinate, as a focus of the people's loyalty and allegiance, continued, albeit under significantly altered conditions, throughout the nineteenth century.[21]
We shall consider below Samson Raphael Hirsch's conception
of the political role of the rabbi in the community.

In addition to a loss of communal and cultural power,
German Orthodoxy found itself increasingly estranged from
the traditionalist masses of Eastern Europe. Insofar as
Orthodoxy per se was a religious-ideological adaptation to the

changing conditions of pre- and post-Emancipation Jewish life, Western Orthodox Jews came to occupy a different cultural environment from East European traditionalists. This process of differentiation, well documented in the works of Jacob Katz, began in the late eighteenth century.[22]

German Orthodox Jews thus faced a double problem: how to compensate for or overcome the cultural domination of heterodox Jews in defining the Jewish situation and how to overcome the impact of the historical process which had created distinct and discrepant Jewries. The basic problem was pluralism. Pluralism was apprehended as the end product of a double exile: the exile of the Jews in the wilderness of history and the exile of the Jewish polity, exacerbated by recent history, from its ontological source of legitimation.

Despite its advanced acculturation into the German middle classes, Orthodoxy held, in a certain sense, to a largely premodern political philosophy. Unlike liberal Judaism, Orthodoxy was not prepared to relinquish Jewish law as the *constitutional* framework for the Jewish polity. Fidelity to halakha implied not simply a personal observance of traditional strictures, but a communal conformity of public institutions with Torah precepts. Frankfurt Orthodoxy, from Samson Raphael Hirsch on, continued to insist on the need for halakha to legitimate the Jewish polity per se.[23] The *Gemeinde* is not a natural fact deriving from the inherent political nature of man as a *zoon politikon*: it is a divine dispensation that provides a model for a comprehensive public/private life. The *Gemeinde* is only a *Gemeinde* when it is founded on a constitution in the Platonic sense: only in the correct order of the polity, can the soul find its order and its perfection. Such a constitution can only be provided by the Torah. Both Orthodox communal separatism (*Austritt*) and Agudah need to be viewed in the terms of a philosophical constitutionalism.

Thus the fact of minority status was more than a demographic problem for the German Orthodox, it was a political-philosophical problem in the most comprehensive sense of the term. Orthodoxy, originally a term of derision applied by the Reform camp, articulated itself into a philosophically fit opponent of liberalized Judaism. As Robert Liberles has shown, Orthodoxy proved its vigor in the nineteenth century by aggressively counterattacking Reform initiatives in the political sphere vis a vis the German state, as well as in developing its own educated subculture and institutions.[24] But, as Liberles's account of Orthodox institution building suggests, the battle between Orthodoxy and Reform was never merely a matter of ideas. It was a battle over the organization and legitimation of the Jewish polity. Ideas are rendered credible, the sociology of knowledge tells us, when the organization of society supports them. When Orthodoxy lost its commanding and exclusive institutional control over the definition of what constituted a Jewish community, it also lost control over those empirical factors which gave its construction of Judaism cogency. It entered into a situation in which its deepest intuitions about Israel's role in the world were disconfirmed by the ordinary life experiences of Orthodox Jews. More and more, Jewish social life tended to jeopardize Orthodoxy's understanding of community as a sacred embodiment of the transcendent unity of Israel, stretching in unbroken constitutional legitimacy back to Sinai. Community, as it became modern, became, to use Schiller's term as popularized by Weber, "disenchanted." Accordingly, Orthodoxy turned toward a project of building its own resacralized communities in order to compensate for the loss of the integral historic polity.[25] Winning community back from its derogation to a profane phenomenon was a motive behind Agudist action.

SACRED POLITY/SECULAR COMMUNITY

It will be worthwhile at this point to explore the process of disenchantment or secularization in greater conceptual and historical detail. There are, it seems to me, two avenues along which the disenchantment of or, more broadly, the secularization of the Jewish polity occured.[26] On the one hand, there is a specific history, stretching from the late eighteenth into the nineteenth centuries that entails what we term "modernization." This has to do with population shifts from village to urban centers, changes in professional and vocational patterns, integration into German culture and society, and a recasting of Judaism into a denominational or confessional phenomenon. Modernization effectuated secularization in the conventional sense. Historians such as Jacob Katz, Robert Liberles, Steven Lowenstein, Mordechai Breuer and Michael Graetz have analyzed this process in detail and we shall return to their findings in the final part of the chapter.

On the other hand, one may speak of an *incipient* or *intrinsic* process of secularization resident in Jewish political and religious tradition as such. This process entails an immanent dialectic of the political and the anti-political; of the profane and the sacred. This is the dimension of secularization or disenchantment to which Max Weber called attention. In Weber's view, there are elements of rationalization and correlative disenchantment implicit already in the experience of ancient Israel. It is important to attend to this implicit secularization process because it gives us criteria to distinguish what is distinctively modern about the loss of sacred community and what can be said to have limited the sacredness of community all along. We will thereby obtain an inherent or ideal-typical standard with which to understand the Agudist conception of sacred community.

By "disenchantment," I refer to Weber's notion of the spiritual byproduct of rationalization.[27] Rationalization means an increasing coherence and consistency of ideas, associated with an increasing systematization of institutions. Rationalization is promoted by the intellectual strata of cultures such as Confucian mandarins or biblical prophets. Where rationalization progresses, belief in the adventitious, spirit-animated character of the world and confidence in magical means to manipulate it diminishes. It is important to note that this is by no means only a modern process, although it has undergone its greatest expansion in modernity. When an ethical, righteous God, for example, replaced a world of competing spirits or nature divinities, rational action, i.e. ethics, replaced magic. Only in the West, under the impact of Israelite monotheism, did a consistently anti-magical worldview prevail. In the most advanced stage of rationalization, the world of western science, disenchantment has become total.[28] It is Weber's thesis that Judaism intuited the possibility of the complete disenchantment of the world.[29]

Unlike the great ancient cultures of the East, the Jews did not produce contemplative mystics, but "inner worldly ascetics." (By "inner-worldly asceticism," Weber implies a religious type of historically-conscious, sober, activist piety centered on the fulfillment in history and society of the divine will. Contemplative mysticism and inner-worldly asceticism are ideal types which permit comparative analysis of religious groups.) The Jews conceived of man as an instrument for purposive action, not as a vessel for salvific, unitive experience. Doing the divine will through a rationally elaborated system of commandments, rather than ruminating on the meaning of the universe as a whole marked Jewish religiosity. "The only problems which could arise were those which were concrete and topical and concerned action in the world; any other problem was excluded."[30]

Thus the process of disenchantment/rationalization is deeply embedded in ancient Judaism's worldview. This does not imply, of course, that Judaism's experience of the sacred was thereby diminished. Rather, for Weber, it was set into a different register from a magical or sacramental experience of the sacred. The sacred was apprehended as action in accordance with the will of an ethical, covenanting God and not as absorption in mysterious Being. Ritual, at least in terms of the prophetic type of Israelite piety, is oriented away from participation in the divine and oriented toward service to his will. *Action* is oriented toward ethical and religious values and invites a high degree of rational analysis and systematization in order to attain conformity with the will of God.

I am making use here of Weber's analysis of the four types of social action: instrumentally-oriented action, value-oriented action, affectually-oriented action, and traditionally-oriented action.[31] Orientation, in Weber's sense, draws attention to the conscious or intended component of action; that is, to the meaning with which the actor endows the action. Action is distinguished from behavior by the criterion of intentionality. Of the four types of action, traditionally- and affectually-oriented actions are the least clearly demarcated from behavior. A traditional orientation implies that the actor follows ingrained patterns of action without much conscious reflection on the ends or means of the action. Without some degree of intention or reflection, however, traditionalism would not qualify as action at all, but only as behavior.[32] This is also true of affectually-oriented action, which is action in accordance with powerful moods and feelings.

Value-oriented (*wertrational*) action, however, entails a high degree of intention and reflection. The agent specifies a set of ethical, aesthetic or religious values and consistently organizes his action toward these values both with respect to ends and to means. In instrumentally oriented (*zweckrational*) action, both the ends, means, and consequences are taken into account and weighed according to criteria of utility. The emotional attachment to values typical of value-oriented action (which often overrides strictly rational calculations of advantage) recedes in this type. Consequently, instrumentally-oriented action is the most consistently rationalized or disenchanted form of action. It is the form most typical of modernity; of the famous "voluptuaries without heart" whom Weber said populate the iron cage of modern bureaucratic society.

That Judaism has a tendency toward rational action at all presupposes that Jewish community and polity are not primarily the locus of divine disclosure or revelation as much as they are purely human social orders which correspond most adequately to the divine will. The social order does not mimic the organization or hierarchy of the world of the gods, such that human beings can vicariously or sacramentally participate in divine order through social order. Jewish monotheism excludes this possibility. Nor can God infuse community in a panentheistic way, as is the case in the Church as the body of Christ. Rather, God relates to the Jewish polity as a non-divine, created and human phenomenon through the device of compact or covenant.

Covenant, probably derived from the treaty relations of ancient near eastern states, signifies a form of social relation in which the integrity of each party, in this case God and Israel, remains intact. The human partner, both as individual and as group, does not lose his humanness. Thus we can say that a certain sphere of unalloyed humanness or legitimated secularity remains foundational to the covenantal social and political order.

Since the radically human dimension of sacred community is not effaced by the covenant, the possibility or the necessity for rational action, both of the instrumental and the value-oriented types, remains a live option. The Torah is not a recipe book that one follows in a behavioral way: decision and choice, *action*, are imperative. Furthermore, action need not always be oriented toward a comprehensive set of sacred norms: freedom is given to humans to devise their own procedures within the broad parameters set by the divine will. The Bible, for example, presents several different models of government: prophetic leadership, confederation, charismatic and dynastic kingship, hierocracy. What God, as it were, insists on is that the polity under any given regime lives up to the norms of the covenant. The choice of regime per se is contingent on historical conditions and human discretion.[33] Here is an instance of the tension, to which I referred above, between the freedom to create social structures, that is, politics, and the demand that that activity be bounded and legitimated by sacred norms. At any rate, the possibility of the disenchantment of community resides in the invitation to rational decision and action. Politics entails disenchantment. Secularization is entailed by the logic of the covenant per se.

We must hasten, however, to avoid overstating this tendency toward incipient secularization. There is, as I have suggested, a dialectic at work. There are strong countervailing forces present in the tradition which hold these tendencies, to a greater or lesser degree, in check. While the covenant concept bears the seeds of secularization, it also and immediately implies a conception of sacral peoplehood which mitigates the secularizing potential of the rational action legitimated by covenantalism. The very people who are affirmed in their human separateness from God are elevated and transformed by their intimacy with him.

Covenant thus entails two polar conceptions of the nature of Jewish peoplehood. These can be analytically distinguished but are, for the most part, implicated in one another. The pole we have emphasized up until now implies an historical, political, and consensual framework. The people and the polity are properly founded through the covenant-making act. This is a political, historical event (that is, it is at least remembered as an historical event) which issues into an empirical state of affairs: a unique, national polity. The book of Exodus largely supports this conceptual framework. The other, countervailing conception instantiated by covenant favors an organic, essentialist model of people and polity with strong transcendent and mythic dimensions. Israel is not merely an historic party to an historic event. It is an eternal archetype whose cosmic destiny requires union with Torah, the eternal cosmic law. Given such an approach, the mundane, empirical, and political aspects of Israel as covenant partner, both at the level of the individual Jew and at the level of the community, retreat before a more sublime synthesis. The organic conception uses corporeal and corporative language which blurs the distinctions between the individual human members of the community, the human side of the covenant and the human/divine dichotomy as such. The Mekhilta de-Rabbi Ishmael expresses this view succinctly:

> The people of Israel are compared to a lamb. What is the nature of a lamb? If it is hurt in one limb, all its limbs feel pain. So also are the people of Israel. One of them commits a sin and all of them suffer from the punishment. But the nations of the world are not so. One of them may be killed and yet all the others may rejoice at his downfall. (Tractate Ba-Hodesh, ch. 2)[34]

The organic, essentialistic conception of Israel assumes a reified Jewish people. The Jewish people are a body; the individual is a limb.[35] This theological framework has profound consequences for the phenomenology of community: it locates the empirical Jewish community in a transcendent context. The local Jewish community is an embodiment of an eternal, metahistorical Israel, an Israel which participates in the heavenly, ideal Israel: *k'nesset Israel*. *K'nesset Israel* is empirical Israel's hypostatic counterpart which argues her case before the divine throne.[36] The empirical community is an instance of Israel's eternal character or *eidos*. *K'nesset Israel* both transcends and participates in all concrete communities. It mediates between empirical Israel and God. The individual and the community participate in this metaphysical *k'nesset Israel* through sacred acts, such as repentance.[37] Following Durkheim, we might say that the community has fashioned a sacred representation of itself in order to locate itself in a sacred cosmos. This *eidos* provides it with access to the sacred center of the cosmos and lends transcendent validity to the norms, customs and practices of the society.

The essentialist, corporative orientation bears specific political consequences. If the institutions of an empirical Jewish community, for example the medieval *kehillah*, are thought to express a transcendent, meta-historical or metaphysical reality, then they stand in an unbroken line of symbolic succession with prior, hallowed institutions and regimes. The *kehillah* inherits the mantle of the biblical *edah* and of the Second Commonwealth Sanhedrin. Leadership is validated in an ontological and symbolic, rather than a rational way. The leaders of the *kehillah* descend symbolically from the Davidic kings, exilarchs and *gaonim*. An outstanding rabbinic leader of the Prague community, Rabbi Jehuda ben Bezalel Loew (1520–1609) expressed this pointedly when he stated that, "the relationship of the rabbi to the community ought to be like that of a king to his subjects . . . As a king rules his subjects, so should the rabbi be the ruler of his constituency."[38]

But clearly there is a difference. Post-biblical authority is authority given in a time of the eclipse of God. While the Davidic dynasty was founded on explicit divine covenant, the exilarchs could only claim derivative divine sanction as their biological descendents. Later Jewish leaders, lacking even this tenuous tie however, presented themselves as *natural* lead-ers, that is, as the natural aristocracy of an organic community which tended toward a natural hierarchy of excellence.[39] The leaders best understand the real interests of the people. They best represent the eternal solidarity of Israel and orient it toward its eschatological goal of salvation.[40]

In fact, the rabbis did try to ground their own authority on biblical sanction both explicit (e.g., the activity of their precursor, Ezra the Scribe) and implied (e.g., the chain of charismatic succession of M. Avot 1:1), but they employed this "naturalistic" line of argument as well. The rabbis thought of themselves as the natural leadership: the group with the most suitable, transcendentally validated qualifica-tions to lead. They embody an institutionalization of charisma that claims more than rationally legitimated excellence for itself. Such a view is anti-political in the sense outlined above. Leadership does not require the real or empirical consent of the citizen. The leaders participate in the transcendental order; the citizen is obligated to acquiesce to their dictates because they embody the supernal truths on which the polity is based.

The politically-oriented, historical-consensual conception, by contrast, understands Israel as an historical artifact, born of deliberation and decision. Israel becomes Israel only by choosing and consenting to covenant. The community is not a reified instance of a reified Israel, but an existential partnership among its members. On the consensual view, Israel becomes Israel because it chooses the path of fidelity to God through the Sinai covenant. Non-Israelites, such as the "mixed multitude" (Exod. 12:38) and Ruth are free to associate themselves with this uniquely composite "nation" if so inclined. Community (*Gemeinschaft*) is based on belief (*Glaubensgemeinschaft*).

The historical-consensual view accepts the contingent status of Israel. Just as Israel retains its strictly human, his-torical identity over/against the divine in the covenantal trans-action, so too do the individual Israelites maintain their indi-viduality over/against the nation. A text from the same tractate of the Mekhilta cited above, commenting on the act of covenanting at Sinai, has it that:

When they all stood before mount Sinai to receive the Torah they all made up their mind alike to accept the reign of God joyfully. Furthermore, they pledged themselves for one another. And it was not only concerning overt acts that God, revealing Himself to them, wished to make His covenant with them but also concerning secret acts, as it is said: "The secret things belong to the Lord Our God and the things that are revealed" (Deut. 29:28). But they said to Him: Concerning overt acts we are ready to make a covenant with Thee, but we will not make a covenant with Thee in regard to secret acts lest one of us commit a sin secretly and the entire community be held responsible for it. (Tractate Ba-Hodesh, ch. 5)[41]

This text points in an entirely different direction from the earlier citation, (thus illustrating, by the way, how difficult it is to find pure cases of these ideal-typical constructions on the operational level). Although it begins to suggest a total of "sublation" of the individual in an organic, corporative community, it recoils from that position and retains the integrity, that is, the autonomy and accountability of the individual members of the covenant community. I suggest that this model invited and—as an historically operational theory—facilitated a higher degree of rational action, prudence and adaptive experimentation than the organic model. It was, additionally, more open to the disenchanting potential of covenantalism.

To the extent that one can speak of two distinct frameworks for the symbolic self-representation of the Jewish people and the Jewish polity, one can only do so at the level of ideal types. The reality is far more mixed. As we have seen, the very concept of covenant works in both ideal-typical directions. Biblical covenanting comprehends both frameworks. God's covenant with David (II Samuel 7), for example, founds an eternal dynasty linked to a mountain of cosmic significance. Two sacred foci, the spatial focus of the Temple and the temporal focus of the Davidic messiah are related to this covenant. God discloses himself on the mountain (that is, in the Temple) and through his fidelity to the dynasty. Here covenanting itself points toward the cosmic.[42]

Simultaneously however, God gives David permission to pursue prudential and rational courses of action, albeit within prophetically mediated limits. God creates a legitimate sphere of secularity where action, legitimated by covenant, may be oriented in an instrumental way. At the same time, however, such action must also be ethically rational with respect to divine norms. Should it fail to conform to these norms, divinely appointed prophets will remind the ruler that his sphere of legitimate secularity is limited by a sacred ring. Secularizing tendencies are kept in check by the theological factors which provide ontological legitimation for the polity.[43]

Let us carry these categories forward in time and focus now on the traditional Ashkenazi community of the European Middle Ages which was the predecessor and nostalgic ideal for the Agudist ideologues of Frankfurt. We will begin with a consideration of the normative roots of the kehillah in the Talmud, as we seek to understand the relative balance of sacred and secular elements in its symbolic self-representation over the course of its history.

As autonomous Jewish polities (kehillot) were in formation in the northern Europe of the tenth century rabbinic leaders, such as Rabbi Meshullam ben Kalonymus and Rabbenu Gershom, sought for elements in the stock of political tradition that would give legitimate authority, both halakhic and symbolic, to the nascent institutions. The Talmud provided few clues. The chief reason for this was that the Talmudic corpus, compiled in Babylonia under conditions of the hierarchical rule of the Exilarch, did not provide precedents for autonomous communities. The Babylonian Talmud presupposed some form of central authority and, in Yitzhak Baer's view, "deliberately downplayed the autonomous authority of the community and refused to recognize its corporate status."[44] Baer believes that the growth of kehillot on the European frontier far from the Jewish centers of Babylonia and Israel represented a reemergence of old traditions of local, public authority.

However this may be, two legitimating strategies, by no means entirely distinct from one another, emerged. According to the first view, the community has powers of compulsion over its members because it is like a court which has the power to impose fines and other punishments. According to the second view, the community represents a partnership—a covenantal relationship—among its members. The community compels because its members have consented to its laws and policies. Both of these views are anticipated in the following Talmudic text:

> Mishna: They compel him to build a gatehouse and a door for a courtyard . . . They compel to build a wall for the city and double doors and a crossbar . . . How long must one be in the city to be as a citizen of the city? Twelve months. Were one to acquire a dwelling, one becomes a citizen immediately. (Baba Batra 7b)

The text presupposes Jewish communities at both a neighborhood and a municipal level. The neighbors in the courtyard or the citizens of the polity can compel their fellows to comply with regulations aimed at improving the safety or privacy of the residents. Both the source or legitimacy of these regulations and the executive power of coercion are left unclear.

In the course of the gemara's discussion of the text, another mishnah (Peah 8:7), as well as an extra-mishnaic statement (baraita), is introduced in order to enumerate further powers of the community. We learn that a community can have two kinds of welfare support (monetary grants and a daily soup kitchen) for the resident as well as the itinerant poor (Baba Batra 8b). Funds for the community chest are collected by two officials, but disbursed by three. Why the asymmetry? The tax assessment of the individual citizen is a matter of public record, so only two officials are required to collect it. (One keeps the other honest.) The disbursal however requires an application of judgment and reason that goes beyond a purely administrative procedure. Disbursal entails a form of "means testing." The panel of three is derived by analogy to a court. Just as a court makes careful decisions about a litigant's status, so too the officials in charge of disbursement must establish how many dependents a poor man has, and so on. Here is one source of the analogization of a community to a court.

By analogizing the community to the court, medieval authorities found an implicitly biblical warrant for their *kehillot*. Sources such as Deuteronomy 16:18 and 17:8–9 require that courts of justice be established in Israel. While the first source is clearly restricted to the public institutions of the future Israelite state, the second turns suggestively to a vaguer future. ("You shall . . . appear before . . . the magistrate in charge at that time and present your problem.") The rabbis used this opening to legitimate their own authority as magistrates appropriate to the times.[45] Moreover, basing themselves on Ezra 10:8 in which the scribe threatens to ban and expropriate the property of Judeans who do not follow his decree and divorce their gentile wives, the rabbis invested courts with legislative and other powers over individual members of the community, such as those of confiscation of property and expulsion.[46] The court therefore provided a reasonable prototype, grounded in divine decree, for the authority of medieval Jewish public institutions. Insofar as much of what they had to do was farm tax revenue from their members, the expropriatory power of the court provided an apt precedent.[47]

Analogizing the community to a court and thereby vesting it with legislative and expropriatory powers was a bold move toward engendering a rational basis for communal policy making. On the other hand, the political empowerment of the communal leadership or the communal majority could only be won by establishing a transcendent ground for such powers. The rabbis, as constitutional interpreters, needed to legitimize the authority of the community and validate its work. This they did through midrashic exegesis and continual oversight of communal decisions.[48] Thus in face of a system that enabled the political action of "citizens" (*bnei ha-ir*) there was a necessary counter-thrust in the direction of traditionalism. Law by its nature must subsume the novel under the precedential, delimiting the sphere of the experimental. It seeks to find and apply rules, not to create policies de novo. The politics of the community as court veers into administration. Mannheim distinguished these two in the following manner:

> At any moment of socio-political life two aspects are discernible—first, a series of social events which have acquired a set pattern and recur regularly; and, second, those events which are still in the process of becoming, in which, in individual cases, decisions have to be made that give rise to new and unique situations . . . When, in the accustomed life of an official, current business is disposed of in accordance with existing rules and regulations, we are . . . in the realm of "administration" rather than of "politics."[49]

Administration has to do with the settled sphere of rule, regulation and precedent. It is the most highly ordered realm of society. Politics, by contrast, has to do with action vis a vis the irrational matrix in which this rationalized sphere is suspended. Whereas administration requires fidelity to established authoritative procedure, politics calls for innovation, choice, experimentation, and prudence. The disenchanting power of politics is great: the magic circle of administrating sacred norms is broken by the possibility of recourse to free, practical reason. Political action threatens the sufficiency of the sacred canopy since it assumes that the human world is characterised by novelty. History is relatively fluid and requires taking risks. All the options for action are not foreordained. Taking risks in the face of what is defined as essentially novel invites anomie. From the point of view of the risk taker, the world appears unstable, undetermined. Living at the margin, one may come to doubt that the traditional cosmos is as integrated as it appears from the center.

The tension between politics and administration becomes fully apparent as the *gemara* proceeds. Given the actuality of two types of welfare fund, cash and food, the gemara adduces that the citizens are permitted to convert the assets of one into the other as need requires. Furthermore, *bnei ha-ir* are permitted to fix weights and measures, prices for basic commodities and workers' wages, as well as to impose fines in order to compel compliance with these decisions. This appears to open the door to a fully empowered citizenry capable of making political and economic decisions on an ad hoc basis. The subsequent discussions of talmudic commentators on this section revolved precisely around this point: to what extent were the citizens free to make decisions? To what extent do halakhic norms restrict decision making ability? For example, can the cash assets of the communal chest be diverted for any public project or only for those projects that benefit the poor? The issue turns on whether politics, in the sense of creative human response to the "irrational matrix" of social circumstances, is fully legitimate or whether the administrative application of established divine norms is in principle sufficient to sustain the sacred system.[50]

The tension comes to a head in the *gemara's* discussion at Baba Batra 9a. A case is introduced to test whether townspeople may indeed set up a political structure wherein fines may be leveled at those who dissent from communal policies. The case entails a professional association, a guild of butchers, who decide to limit their competition insofar as all of them cannot make a living without some measure of cooperation and coordination of their business activity. They designate days of the week on which each may slaughter. Should one slaughter on another's day, the others then have the right to confiscate the hide of the slaughtered animal and tear it (rendering it valueless), thus fining in effect the butcher who dissented from the agreement of the partnership. This occurred, and the butcher who was so fined appealed to a leading sage, Rava, against the butchers for restitution. Rava agreed that the terms of the partnership were not binding and ordered the others to compensate the butcher.

Another (lesser) sage, Rav Yeimar, challenged Rava by citing the *baraita* that townspeople can impose fines to compel compliance with public ordinances. Rava keeps an aloof silence, deigning not to answer Rav Yeimar. Who then is right,

Rava or Rav Yeimar? The *gemara* sides with Rava, explaining that the principle of the autonomy of the townspeople is effective *only* when there is no distinguished man, that is, rabbinic sage, to make public decisions. Rava was such a man. Not wishing to make a show of his authority, he kept a humble silence before Rav Yeimar. Although the *gemara's* rule that a distinguished man, an "administrator" of the sacred in our sense, must validate communal policies was challenged by later halakhic authorities, it does illustrate the persistent tendency to restrain the political that is inherent in the system.[51]

Thus the text decisively limits the sphere of the political through the force of the administrative. The sage's action, which is traditionally or ethically oriented, outweighs the merely political, instrumental action of the townsmen. The secular is overwhelmed by the urge for the sacral. The *gemara's* implication seems to be that rule by sages is more legitimate than self-rule. Talmudic community was regulated by rabbinic administrators representing the central institutions of the gaonate and the exilarchate. Polity was not conceived of as a self-regulating partnership between citizens. Indeed, such a conception of citizenship represents a Greek ideal, not a rabbinic one. Even after *kehillot*, which were effectively self-regulating partnerships, came into being, the rabbis, who were charged with positing and reflecting on the grounds of their presumptive legitimacy, tended largely to view the partnership model as a secondary tradition, without the full legitimacy of the community as court.[52]

By and large then, the tradition favored the court model and, if not the rule, at least the confirmation of public policy by the sages. Yet to speak of "rule by sages" and of the community as a court does not undermine the basically republican premisses of the Jewish polity. The people own the institutions of the polity, they are not the private preserve of a ruling family, dynasty, or class. While the rabbis form a natural aristocracy of learning and virtue, membership in their "estate" is in principle open to all males. Furthermore, their charisma may be natural, but their authority *derives* from the community.[53] The leaders, whether they were rabbis themselves or whether they ruled with the collaboration of rabbis, were appointed by their communities and were responsible to them. They did not own the community; they represented it.

The issue of the symbolic self-representation of the polity is closely related to the issue of power within the community. The leaders represented the community in a double, distinctively medieval, sense. On the one hand, they represent the sovereign will of the community which installed them. They are there to execute the community's wishes. So far, the republican premise of the Jewish political tradition. On the other hand, as the natural aristocracy of the community, they best represent its real and enduring interests. The community itself may be aware only of its *endoxa*, its transient governing opinions. The leaders, however, are aware of the truths by which the community ultimately must live. Consequently, the community must see in the will of its leaders the highest representation of its own will.[54] Rational, political processes of consent matter less than acquiescence to what is ultimately right. This acquiescence is acheived by consent to the will of the leaders who embody what is right. Here we see once again the powerful orientation toward the organic, essentialist conception of Jewish peoplehood and polity refered to above.

The mainline of the tradition, analogizing the community (or at least the representative leadership of the community) to a court, ascribed both judicial and legislative power to the community. Under its legislative aspect, the polity could compel any single individual or a group of individuals, that is, a minority, to follow its dictates. Majority rule derived from the practice of courts. Since the decision-making procedure of Jewish courts was based from ancient times on majority rule, the majority's decision was, given conformity with other norms of the legal system, in principle valid for communal structures as well.[55] Thus minorities were obliged to consent.

The principal dissenter from the prevailing view of the community as court and its weakened implications for consensual politics was Rabbenu Tam. Rabbenu Tam maintained that minorities were not bound to majority decision in advance of their consent, nor were they obligated to consent simply because a majority had enacted a policy.[56] The minority can always withhold its consent because community, in Rabbenu Tam's view, is not like a court. It is, rather, a partnership of its members. Since it is not a court its majoritarian decisions are not indisputably valid. On the surface, Rabbenu Tam appears to support the partnership model with its superior political potential for rational action and its thematization of individual involvement and consent. In fact, however, he does just the opposite. His apparent embrace of the partnership model was just a foil for his own version of rabbinic rule. The force of his view is to disqualify the partnership model with its requirement of maximal consent as an unworkable foundation for communal governance. If everyone has to consent to a communal enactment, how could public business ever be successfully settled?

Actual legislative power, in Rabbenu Tam's view, resides neither in the citizens nor in the community as a court, but in the hands of the greatest scholars of the generation. The leading rabbis act de jure as a body with the same legitimacy as the Sanhedrin.[57] In subsequent legal history, Rabbenu Tam's position was able to be neither sustained nor discarded. Communities throughout the Ashkenazi Middle Ages were unwilling to suspend their old traditions of majority rule and local governance, both of which Tam had called into question. On the other hand, acknowledged sages often acted as supervisors or critics of majority rule thus guarding against the potential abuses inherent in majoritarianism.[58] Rabbenu Tam, while apparently opting for the political approach of the partnership model, actually returned to the talmudic, "administrative" approach. The ultimate ground for the power of the community is the sovereignty of the Torah, interpreted by the leading exponents of the generation.

It is clear then that both in terms of the court and the partnership models, the underlying tendency is the same: to delimit the sphere of political action and to maximize sacred, administrative control. Let us turn now from the issue of the symbolic self-representation of the polity to a consideration of its actual workings. We will try to analyze those elements of communal practice which might have promoted a disenchanting view of the polity. We will also consider the forces which, once again, kept disenchantment in check.

As the Jewish political tradition works itself out in the European Middle Ages, the rabbis do not act as the sole leaders of their communities. Both rabbis and "laymen" have complementary shares in the governance of the community. The *kehillot* developed well-defined institutional structures with several tiers of appointed volunteer and salaried leadership, as well as formalized mechanisms for retaining and compensating rabbis.[59] Rabbis and notables (*parnassim*) worked together in a mutually supportive constitutional arrangement. Although their basic orientations, at the level of ideal types were in tension, in reality competition between the two groups was minimized insofar as they shared a consensus about the Torah as the ultimate ground of public life.

While tensions undoubtedly existed between lay policy makers and rabbis, both needed one another. They coexisted in mutually supportive legitimacy. The laymen accepted that Torah, by providing a system of religious values to which action must conform, delimited the range of free political action. Even those agents who had relative freedom of action within the *kehillah*, such as the top elected officers who had a free hand for the duration of their terms or the *shtadlan*, who dealt with the mysterious and changeable world of the gentiles, regulated themselves by the consensual values.[60]

This pervasive agreement on constitutional first principles minimized the differences between rabbis and lay officers of the polity, casting them as complementary agencies of the same organism. Communal policies and ordinances were drafted by committees of lay officers (*ba'alei takkanot*) generally with, but sometimes without rabbinic involvement. The rabbi was, at any rate, often obliged to sign the *takkanot*, thus symbolically securing their conformity with the meta-norms of Torah and halakha.[61] Although dependent on the community for his position and commission, the rabbi served as a medium which related the periphery to the sacred center, the social body to its transcendent source. The community was dependent upon the rabbi for its ontological legitimation. Thus one potential source of the secularizing or disenchanting potential of instrumental, practical rationality—the conflict between laymen and rabbis—was kept within bounds by the constitutional consensus of the premodern Jewish community.

If what we have termed politics was relatively restricted by a normative consensus and by the impulse toward administration, what about the rationalization of administration per se? An increasing routinization of administrative procedures, even if originally sanctified as halakhically valid *takkanot* or as timeless custom (*minhag*) might have a disenchanting effect. Social action under such circumstances could be oriented to sustaining and maximizing the procedures themselves, rather than to realizing the values they enshrine. By the sixteenth century, for example, *kehillot* acquired a highly differentiated system of officers attending to a customary division of labor. Although these positions were elected and voluntary, the officials often employed paid functionaries, thus bringing a veritable bureaucracy into being.[62] There were professional street sweepers, prison wardens, town scribes and so on. Their wages were fixed by *takkanah*. A ramified and rationalized administrative system, such as the large *kehillot* developed, curtailed both direct participatory democracy and the dependence on direct charismatic authority. Public institutions were independent of their holders. Leading families or rabbis, influential as they might have been, were nonetheless perceived as separate from their positions. This degree of rationalization must have occasioned a sense of disenchantment. A world where the appointment of a communal rabbi was a regularized business procedure is a world where appointments can be bought. Rabbis could pay for their positions, enjoy a monopoly on rabbinic functions in the *kehillah* and win a return on their investment.[63] As Jacob Katz points out, this stabilization and professionalization of the rabbinate came at a price: the rabbi's increasing centrality meant that he could be blamed for the failures of the *kehillah*.[64] But there must have been another cost as well: the institutionalization of charisma implies the attenuation of charisma. By the eighteenth century, the authority of the communal rabbinate had declined considerably.[65]

It is therefore at least arguable that the very success of the adminstrative dynamic within the traditional community held within it a potential for partial secularization. This tendency must have been kept in check by continual reference to constitutional first principles, to the ultimate Torah values which the community believed itself to represent. The consensus on those values was reenacted in and sustained by daily life. The *kehillah*, regardless of how rationalized its public life had become, nonetheless continued to participate organically in the eternal, transcendent reality of *knesset Israel*. The continuing segregation and isolation from the gentile world closed the *kehillah* off as a world unto itself. Its deepest intuitions about itself as the sacred Jewish polity, albeit in exile from the sacred land, were confirmed by its social situation. When this consensual worldview failed, as it did in the German communities of the nineteenth century, the latent secularity of administrative practice became actual.

An additional factor must have infringed upon the numinous quality of the sacred community: the reality of power. The medieval rise and the early modern decline of the *kehillah*, although certainly expressing forces immanent in the Jewish political tradition, was largely dependent on the dynamics of gentile governments. When it suited their purposes to allow *kehillot* to develop, as, for example, efficient agencies of tax farming, they did not hinder their development. When, on the other hand, the modern, centralizing state wanted to abolish medieval structures such as the *kehillah*, *kehillot*, and supra-*kehillah* organizations were dismantled.[66] The dependence of Jewish authority on gentile power could of course be rationalized as part of the divine plan of the exile. The reality of this situation, at least among those who enjoyed such derivative authority, must have deflated somewhat the *kehillah's* traditional discourse of the sovereignty of the Torah.[67] In addition, there was the reality of power within the community. Although the *kehillah's* premise was fundamentally republican, its practice was aristocratic, even plutocratic. And although, as we have seen, appeals were made to halakhic precedents, matters which fell to discretion such as the details of taxation policy were often worked out along power lines. Interest groups negotiated with each other for the most favorable results. These hard realities must have strengthened the awareness, or at least raised the suspicion, of the secular character of political thought and practice.

Many of these features are observable in the *takkanot* of the Jewish community of Frankfurt am Main.[69] The community was administered by twelve elected senior officers (*Vorsteher* or *Baumeister*, i.e., *parnassim*). Every month, two of them formed a rotating presidium, thus insuring that each of the twelve would lead the board at least once a year. Frankfurt's city council, as well as the Holy Roman Emperor, gave the officers a broad range of powers. The Jewish regulation (*Stättigkeit*) of 1616, for example, granted them the authority to punish those who defied their *takkanot* with fines and the ban. They promulgated *takkanot*, supervised the community's finances in conjunction with another level of officers (the *Kastenmeister*, i.e., *gabaim*), administered public works, acted in loco parentis for orphans and represented the community to the gentiles. Their power was limited only by the duration of their terms and by their internal rivalries. These top officials formed a political class. The same family names repeat again and again in the statute book. They were a natural aristocracy, drawn from the wealthiest members of the community. Although electoral procedures permitted almost every class to participate, in practice, the wealthy monopolized the sphere of politics for themselves. This was not, however, apprehended as an unnatural state of affairs, for an era of citizenship and mass political participation had not yet dawned.

In conclusion, it seems fair to say that rationalizing tendencies existed in the Jewish political tradition from the beginnings of covenantalism through the epochs of Talmudic culture. Jewish political life in the Middle Ages exemplifies the tension between a rationally oriented politics and a traditionally oriented moralism, but this tension, with its disenchanting potential, was moderated by agreement about constitutional first principles and, fundamentally, by the reality of exclusion from the outside world. Since the Jews were, by force and by choice, a "people that dwells apart," their social situation confirmed their symbolic self-representation.

THE IDEALIZATION OF THE SACRED POLITY: SAMSON RAPHAEL HIRSCH AND HIS FOLLOWERS

The modern age, in contrast to its predecessor epoch, was a time when the disenchanting and centrifugal forces latent in the community spun out of control. Polity, as we have seen, became community. That is, the *kehillah* with its law making and coercive powers and its obligatory membership gradually became a voluntaristic community. Indeed, this process was slower in Germany than in other European countries and the obligation to belong to the local *Gemeinde* remained intact until 1876. But this obligation was perceived not as an inner necessity, but as a coercive policy of the state, at least by the most traditional members of the community. The inner conviction that the *Gemeinde* was a *kehillah kedoshah*, a holy community, had failed. Thus, by the early nineteenth century, broad agreement on what I have called constitutional first principles was lacking. The Frankfurt Orthodox believed they had to reconstruct the sacred polity in the midst of the secularized *Gemeinde*.

The means that they used to accomplish this were distinctly modern. Until they won the legal right of secession in 1876, the leading Orthodox families formed a society (*Religionsgesellschaft*) from 1850 on within the officially recognized community.[70] As Michael Graetz has argued, creating voluntary societies (*Vereine*) was a distinctly modern, Enlightenment approach to the decline of the statutory community. The *kehillah* had always had its voluntary subgroups (*ḥavurot*), often with their own constitutions and special sphere of activity. These *ḥavurot* were classic mediating institutions in that they gave their members a sense of belonging and a sphere of significant activity in a context more immediate than that of the impersonal, aristocratic institutions of the *kehillah*. In the modern context, however, the *Vereine* were not so much mediating institutions, but alternative communities. The *Gemeinde* as a whole was perceived to be not only distant, but no longer supportive or expressive of the values of an Enlightened age or, in the Orthodox case, of a traditional sub-group.

Given the reality of a distinctly modern medium, that is, the *Verein*, for the expression of their religio-social values, the Orthodox had also to overcome the dimension of secularity implicit in the framework they chose. Indeed, we might say, if the above analysis is correct, that they had to negate the dimension of secularity, of "politics" implicit in the tradition all along. They had to imagine themselves in possession of a structure that was not only more than a mere *Verein*, but was also more sacred than the *kehillah* that had been lost. Of course, they would not have known that the *kehillah* had its incipiently secular tendencies insofar as the living reality of the *kehillah* had long before expired. Their's is a utopian reconstruction of a *kehillah* that never quite existed. The immediacy of a living tradition had been lost. It was replaced, in Menachem Friedman's terminology, by the artificiality of a "book tradition."[71]

This utopianism marks their project as distinctly modern. As Robert Liberles suggests, whereas the old community depended on natural ties of kinship, the alternative community of the Israelitische Religionsgesellschaft (IRG) depended upon consent to a cohesive, rationally articulated worldview.[72] The need to reestablish the prominence and the purity of constitutional first principles led to an emphasis on the rational design of institutions, and of their rational justification. At the same time, these ideas were not thought to be progressive, but merely restorative. Thus the utopianism of Frankfurt

Orthodoxy was marked by both conservative and liberal-humanitarian tendencies.

In Karl Mannheim's typology, liberal-humanitarian utopianism implies a system of ideas which provide a set of goals for the achievement of the ideal society.[73] Yet, typically for the liberal schema, the ideal is not believed to be strictly regulative and futuristic. It is understood to reside in what is, to be immanent in the real. Thus the real, especially that which is inherited via tradition, has sacred worth. Social reality is believed to be sufficiently tractable so as to be able to conform to the system of ideas and ideas are not alien to reality because reality is believed to be fundamentally rational. In the more conservative form in which we encounter this mentality here, we might say that ideas are not alien to reality because their normative force already inheres in the reality of sacred tradition. The utopian mentality strives to bring reality into line with the immanent, yet ideal social design. The conservative and liberal utopian mentalities fuse insofar as the essential content of the tradition is itself articulated in a rational fashion.

Given this rationalistic optimism, the religion of the Frankfurt Orthodox has strongly rationalistic traits. There is an avoidance, at least in Samson Raphael Hirsch, of Jewish mysticism as both a system of speculation and of practice. Positively, the tradition is construed largely in legal and ethical categories as a system of rationally defensible duties leading to the completion and perfection of man and society. Hirsch's is an essentially liberal, post-Kantian theology oriented toward supporting the traditional Jewish way of life. As such, Hirsch scrupulously avoids any form of chiliasm, ecstasy or asceticism. The principle focus of his thought is the Torah as the constitution of an ideal society and as the guide to moral perfection.[74]

These tendencies come to the fore in Hirsch's principle essay on community. His views on community are found in an 1855 essay published in the first issue of his journal, *Jeshurun*. The name of the journal, like the exegesis which forms the core of the essay, relates to Deuteronomy 33:4–5:

Moses taught us Torah; an inheritance of the community of Jacob (*kehillat Jacob*). And there will be a king in Jeshurun when the heads of the people assemble together with the tribes of Israel.

This verse had a crucial weight in Hirsch's thought. Indeed, it also became, as we shall see, the kernel of Agudat Israel's political theology. In Hirsch's understanding, the verse points toward both the normative constitutional principle of the Jewish community in the present, and toward the full messianic realization of the principle in the future. (That is to say, utopia consists in the full implementation of the system of ideals fully discernible but only partially realized in the present.) The principle is that Torah is sovereign in the community. The community exists only in order to fulfill the Torah, to enable the individual to fulfill his Torah duties better than he could in isolation and to give concrete social expression to the Torah's design for a kingdom of priests and a holy nation.[75]

Hirsch opts for the view that the Torah rather than God, on the one hand, or Moses, on the other, is sovereign. In his exegesis, he maintains (somewhat against the grammar of the two verses) that it is Torah which becomes the king in Jeshurun when the people are properly assembled. Furthermore, the people can only be properly assembled, that is, they can only constitute a community, when Torah is their king. In identifying the king of the community with Torah, Hirsch departs somewhat from the teaching of the major traditional exegetes. The leading exegetes entertained three positions: that God is king, that Moses is king, and that Torah is king.

Rashi, for example, states tersely that the reference to the future king in Jeshurun is the "Holy One, Blessed be He."[76] Ibn Ezra, on the other hand, maintains that "king" is not a future-oriented, eschatological reference, but refers contemporaneously to Moses, who teaches the people Torah and gathers the leaders of the people to him in order to instruct them. Ibn Ezra, however, cites what he considers a minority view, the teaching of Yehuda Halevi, who, like Hirsch after him, infers that the verse refers to the kingship of the Torah. Halevi's view implies that Israel can have no king other than Torah.

Nachmanides, like Rashi, believes that king refers to God, who will rule when the people accept the Torah which Moses teaches them. God's kingship will be in place when the people uphold the unchangeable and eternal Torah. Nachmanides explicitly rejects the attribution of kingship to Moses. He also makes it clear that the Torah is an instrument of divine sovereignty and not the locus of divine sovereignty per se.

Why did Hirsch side with the counterintuitive, minority position? I suggest he did so because it best accorded with the rationalist cast of his thought. The main thrust of his essay is to argue that in order for the Torah to become king, the entire community must become involved in the study of Torah. As is well known, Hirsch promulgated a *Bildungsideologie*, a philosophy of education. He advocated a synthesis between traditional Jewish learning and modern secular studies under the banner of *"Torah im derekh eretz,"* the mutual ennoblement of Torah and general culture. His success as a propagandist for Orthodoxy lay in his attractive fusion of the Enlightenment quest for self-perfection through mental cultivation (*Bildung*)—an ideal embraced by the majority of German Jews—with the traditional demand of Torah study (*talmud torah*).[77] In the present essay, Hirsch argues that the rejuvenation of authentic Jewish community life will only take place when the "fire-law" of the Torah (cf. Deut. 33:2) becomes the animating principle of each individual life and of the collective purpose.[78]

By stressing the centrality of Torah and the obligation for all to be involved in its study, Hirsch calls attention to the constitutional role of Torah: the people, its land, and its state exist only to fulfil the Torah.[79] Furthermore, the community is the local embodiment of the people; it is Israel in miniature, the bearer of Israel's collective tasks.[80] This community, which requires legitimate authority over the individual in order to perform its tasks, acquires such authority only insofar as it complies with Torah, as it promotes the study of Torah.[81] If this is not its animating soul, its organizational body, however healthy it might appear, is inwardly dead.[82]

In Hirsch's view, the constitutional centrality of Torah implies a republican political philosophy. The stress on lay participation in Torah study means that no religious professionalism—the clergy model of Christianity which he blames the Reform Jews for importing into Judaism—is acceptable.[83] The decisions of the rabbi and the elected officers are accepted as authoritative only when the people are imbued with Torah. If the people are not steeped in Torah, the officers elected by them will lack discernment and the rabbi's decisions will be scorned. Hirsch interprets the rabbinic maxim, "raise up many students" (Avot 1:1) as a rule for rabbis: make yourselves superfluous; when all are full of Torah, your leadership will be unnecessary.[84]

A number of strands come together here. What Hirsch is proposing is a complete sublimation of the political dimensions of communal life in a system of sacred administration. The sovereignty of the Torah, the total identification of any authoritative public decision with the dictates of the Torah, subsume the sphere of political action into the routine of administration. Hirsch seems to envision, like other nineteenth century thinkers, the replacement of politics by rational administration. Here is a liberal utopianism, albeit rooted in an incipient tendency of the Jewish political tradition, in full flower. The social reality of the Jews can be ordered according to the sacred ideas of the text as it has been rationally explicated by the sages and their followers. The Religionsgesellschaft is to be the embodiment and the model for this subordination of the uncertain world of politics to the certainties of the sacred canopy.

It is interesting to note that Hirsch minimizes the role of rabbinic authority. His view points in the opposite direction from the Eastern European Orthodox elevation of "daat Torah," the application of charismatic rabbinic authority to contemporary political questions.[85] Hirsch does not present the rabbi as a kind of oracle, but rather as representing the community by expressing those truths of which everyone is (or should be) aware because they underlie the community's consensus. As in the late medieval *kehillah*, the rabbi's authority is strictly derivative. It depends on the will of the community board, on the one hand, and his demonstrable competence in legal matters, on the other. Appeals to a supra-rational charism are out of order.

Hirsch employs what we have termed an empirical or historical model of Jewish community. Drawing perhaps from the social contract tradition of Rousseau, he understands Israel and its public institutions to be a product of decision and choice. The people band together and form authoritative institutions in order to better fulfill the Torah (which they freely accepted) than they could have on their own. The Torah is phenomenologically primary. The community is derivative and instrumental. Yet once composed by covenant or contract, the community has the right to compel its members to continue to acknowledge the basic norm of their collective enterprise. The tradition, according to Hirsch, values mutual compulsion for the public good.[86] Rousseau's tendency toward maximal consensus and his thick view of the common good, expressed in his notion of the *volonte generale* come to mind here.[87]

Hirsch's theory of community, although it employs a social contract model of origins and of political obligation, also resorts to frequent organic metaphors. (As was argued above, the tradition often mixes these different symbolic frames of reference.) The organic unity of Israel, however, is not prior to its involvement with Torah. The ontological priority of Torah occasions and insures the integrity of Israel. By ordering the unity of Israel in this fashion, Hirsch avoids a mystical reification of Israel as such. The Torah remains the ontological fundament, but it is not subject to reification either. Its being in the world resides in its constitutional role in the community, in the maximal consensus it enjoys in the hearts and minds of the members of the community, and in the praxis of *talmud torah*.

The composite unity of Israel, occasioned by and dependent upon Torah, is designated by Rashi and by Nachmanides, in their commentaries on Deut. 33:5, *agudah ahat*, one band or union. God is truly king above when Israel unites in one band below. Nachmanides refers to a cluster of midrashim which expand on this motif.

> *Gather unto Me.* This bears on what Scripture says, *It is He that buildeth His upper chambers in the heaven and hath founded His vault (agudatho) upon the earth* (Amos 9:6). To what may this be likened? To a palace built upon boats. As long as the boats are joined together the palace that is upon them stands. In the same way we can explain *It is He that buildeth His upper chambers in the heaven.* His throne, if one may be allowed the expression, is established on high when Israel form one band (*agudah*). This is the reason why it says, *It is He that buildeth His upper chamber in the heaven.* When does he build it? When He hath founded His agudah upon the earth. In the same strain it says, *And there was a king in Jeshurun* (Deut. 33:5). Accordingly the Holy One, blessed be He, said to Moses: *Gather unto Me.* Why? Because the gathering together of righteous people is a benefit to them and a benefit to the world. The gathering together of wicked people, however, is a stumbling block to them and a stumbling block to the world.[88]

The implication of this text, certainly known to Hirsch and to Rosenheim, is that the establishment of God's reign in both heaven and on earth requires, in no small measure, the organizational unity of the Jewish people. Practical activity—community building—is redemptive activity. The organizational work of overcoming Israel's structural disintegration in exile (*Galut*) will overcome the *Galut* per se. Such premises underlie the choice of the name Agudat Israel. In Jacob Rosenheim's theory of community, more so than in Hirsch's, the full messianic thrust of practical action is evident.

Rosenheim, and Agudat Israel in general, derive much of their orientation from Hirsch's practical and theoretical work. (Indeed, theory and praxis were closely bound together in both Hirsch and Rosenheim.) The emphases on the primacy of educational activity, on lay or, more politically, republican participation in governing and policy formation, the necessity for rabbinic oversight and accreditation of republican governance, and the implicitly salvific dimension of organization are all strongly present in Rosenheim.

Rosenheim's 1929 essay, "Der Agudistische Einheitsgedanke" (The Agudist Conception of Unity) offers a concise exposition of his views. The essay, prepared to give ideological coherence to the 2nd Knessiah Gedolah (Great Assembly) of the organization, seeks to clarify the philosophical and religious convictions that underlie Agudah's practical activity. It wants to raise to consciousness, as it were, the ideas that, in an unarticulated fashion, reside in the day to day praxis. Just as Hirsch believed that the Religionsgesellschaft was nothing other than the ideal and microcosmic form of the nation under present historical circumstances, so Rosenheim believed that the Agudah is nothing other than the organized form of the Torah people in *Galut*.[89] As such, it seeks nothing but the old definition of Israel's essence and task. For Rosenheim, this is found in the Shema (Deut. 6:5): the daily proclamation of God's "upper and lower" unity. The ideal Jewish people and its organized manifestation in the world of secular history (*Kulturwelt*) has no other fundamental task than achieving unification with God and His Torah. Rosenheim calls Agudat Israel to bind itself to the deepest religious sources of its Jewish being (*jüdisches Sein*) and to represent unificatory loyalty to God before the world. He adds that the present time is a time of *ikva d'meshikha* (the anticipation of the messiah), and thus a time to act decisively for the Lord.[90]

How is this unificatory action to be achieved? The daily practice of reciting the Shema provides the Jew with deep ontological insight. The Shema gives Jews the conviction that the plurality and difference of the world masks an inner unity.

The necessity and mechanistic causation of the material universe—which in its inexorability appears to be a god in itself—is penetrated by the Jewish heart, which discovers a world of divine love behind the veil.[91] Interestingly, Rosenheim suggests that modern physics has at last an inkling of this Jewish conviction (which the Jews have kept alive for the rest of the world). The old nineteenth century mechanistic determinism of *Kraft und Stoff* (the title of a popular scientistic work by Buechner) has been exploded by twentieth century particle physics. The border between organic and inorganic life has been erased. Now the entire universe is known to be pulsating with Spirit, which testifies, albeit obliquely, to the apriority of the Creator God.[92]

But the unificatory moment of the Shema cannot remain only on the level of consciousness. Thought flows into deed. The second stage of unification requires actualizing the kingship of God in human history. History resembles nature in that beyond its near infinite plurality, there is a unity. The peoples, not the individual, are the bearers of human history. The peoples and their particular histories represent the robust particularity and difference of history per se. The Jews, however, are the special creation of God within this dazzling, apparently goalless chaos of particularities. They represent the unity of creation, the sign of the one Creator: the telos of this seeming goallessness.[93]

Israel has a cosmological and eschatological task: to represent, indeed, to *effectuate* unification. On this both cosmos and history depend.[94] Rosenheim now introduces a dialectic: unity means overcoming existence at the periphery and finding the center; overcoming individuation and finding completion in an organic whole. Yet individuation must be developed to its highest point before particularity can find its way back to unity. Consequently, the Jewish people—the very sign of unity—is simultaneously a diaspora, that is, a splintered people. The various Jewries are historically individuated and must find their way back to meta-historical unity. All authentic Jewish cultures seek the Jewish whole.[95] Agudat Israel is nothing other than this holy will toward Jewish unity becoming conscious of itself and mobilizing in the midst of human history. Agudat Israel is the form Israel requires as it struggles to become the organic unity (*Einheitsorganismus*) that it was *in illo tempore* and that it will be in the fullness of time. The task of building the Agudah is of such moment that Agudah will be built by God himself. Israel and God will be partners in the work of creation.[96]

Rosenheim's theory of community has a strongly metaphysical orientation. He does not hesitate to ground community in cosmological and eschatological processes. The daily tasks and trials of political life find a sublime justification. Agudat Israel is the very idea of history clarifying itself to itself. In Agudat Israel, being and time find their sacred face. The transformation of community into sacred polity is complete. Secularity and plurality are entirely overcome.

These religious ideas of community and polity developed out of the classical inheritance of the Jewish political tradition. The distinctly cosmological turn of Hirsch and Rosenheim, that is, their placing the community or polity in the center of a spiritually charged universe and investing it with mediatory function vis a vis divine power recalls the organic, essentialistic and archetypal conception of Jewish peoplehood described above.

This preference for organic metaphors to describe Israel's collective nature and character derives both from the classical Jewish inheritance and from the intellectual style of German conservative thought, where organic language was used to counter the liberal Enlightenment concepts of equality, universal rights, and citizenship.[97] Although Hirsch and Rosenheim were political and, in a certain sense, intellectual liberals (i.e., at least with respect to their utopias) the vocabulary of conservatism with its emphasis on the ancient roots of the public world and its hallowed collective way of life was deeply attractive. Conservatism's rejection of individual liberty and its emphasis on liberty as the liberty of the group to develop organically; its penchant for the normativeness of the past, for the past as a template for action in the present fills the thought of Hirsch and Rosenheim.

This new/old self-representation as an archetypal and organic collective stood in stark contrast to the more covenantal/consensual reality, namely, that both the IRG and its outgrowth, Agudat Israel, were really voluntary societies of like-minded individuals pledged to pursue common ideals. Sociologically, they were *Vereine*, private societies which the post-Enlightenment, liberal world created to give meaning to the concept of civil society. Even conservatives who rejected the liberal premises upon which *Vereine* were based could do no better than form them themselves.

The covenantal acts on which the IRG community and the Agudah polity were founded were represented by the founders on another level of discourse entirely. Both the contemporary liberal character of the *Verein* and the traditional pole of consensual covenantalism were swallowed up in a cosmologizing turn. This turn was an attempt to express, using classical religious symbols, their own experience of the power of the sacred center to which they were now, by means of their new institutions, related.

In the next chapter, we will look at the early history of the Agudah movement and consider how its religiously charged self-representation stood up under the stresses and strains of actual political conditions.

Chapter 3

RENEWING THE SACRED POLITY:
THE FOUNDING OF AGUDAT ISRAEL

AN AGE OF ORGANIZATIONS

In his autobiography, Isaac Breuer called the twentieth century the "century of organizations."[1] To state the matter more precisely, we would have to expand the time frame into the middle of the nineteenth century. The second half of the nineteenth century saw an enormous flourishing of Jewish organizational life in England and France, and, somewhat later, in Germany. Modern organizations such as the British Board of Deputies (begun in 1760, but legally recognized in 1836) or the French Alliance Israelite Universelle (1860) represented attempts to carry on Jewish political traditions, for Jewish religious and political purposes, under the changed and changing conditions of Emancipation.[2]

That Jews sought to organize their communal life on a national scale and to create national, indeed, international welfare, defense and other voluntary organizations attests to the tenacity and adaptability of the Jewish political tradition. The nineteenth century was an age of mass politics, of the growth of parties, of the heightened symbolic and actual involvement of broad strata of the population in public decision making. Jews responded to these changes by creating organizations that could, symbolically, present themselves as centers, as representatives of an entire Jewish public.

This urge toward political self-representation qualifies, as Robert Liberles has argued, the standard image of the modernizing, assimilating Western Jew who reduced Judaism to a confession.[3] That these organizations were often dominated by Reform or agnostic Jews attests to the persistence of political traditions, however occluded these traditions might have been by the prevailing Jewish discourse.[4] On the other hand, that the organizations were created and directed by the most modernized Jews, that is, by Jews most influenced by the ideal of *Bildung*, also suggests that these societies served not just as a surrogate for traditional Jewish communal institutions but as an ersatz for traditional piety as well. The secular practice of welfare and defense replaced the religious practice of observance of *mitzvot*. The incipiently secular tendency within the Jewish political experience became stronger as Jewish community became ever more disenchanted.

Emancipation and renewed community building were related enterprises. Modernization was more than assimilation. It entailed political development, that is, the transformation of an integral and sacred Jewish collective existence, under new legal and social realities, into a pluralistic and secular (in the sense of disenchanted) collective existence. Collective existence never lost its importance. Even as religious observance was transformed or diminished, Jews expressed their solidarity with one another and their wish to represent themselves, symbolically and actually, as a collectivity through their organizations. What changed was the symbolic self-definition of the collectivity. The balance between sacred and profane shifted in favor of the later. The mere fact that organizations had a history, that people created them for certain tasks at distinct points in time was inherently disenchanting. The basis on which they were justified or legitimated, while often appealing to sacred grounds, was perforce practical and rational.

The Orthodox organizations, as we have seen, attempted to have it both ways. While appealing to rational criteria to justify their existence, their proponents also gave them mythical depth. Orthodox organizations portrayed themselves as a reemergence of age-old institutions and archetypal traditions that had been nearly lost by emancipation. Hirsch's Israelitische Religionsgesellschaft, the Freie Vereinigung, and Agudat Israel, from an internal point of view, were not so much invented as rediscovered.

Organizations developed both to serve the political and social needs of a modernizing Jewish community and, as we saw earlier in our consideration of the medieval *kehillah*, because they were compatible with the needs and purposes of the state. The British Jews, for example, overcame their internal fissure between Sephardim and Ashkenazim and developed a central representation, the Board of Deputies, in the early nineteenth century. The Board of Deputies was to be the authoritative representative in the struggle for full civic equality. The government recognized it as such in 1836 when it gave the Board authority to certify and to help the state register Jewish marriages. This central organization was viewed by the government as an efficient means of performing administrative tasks during its own period of reform.[5]

In France, by contrast, the initiative for a modernized, centralized communal organization came not only from the Jews themselves, but from the state. Between 1806–1808, Napoleon reorganized the Jewish community into consistories, administrative bodies in the departments with significant Jewish population, presided over by a central council in Paris. The Jews sought public assistance, recognition, and support in order to rebuild their weakened, battered communities. The government sought an efficient means of executing its Jewish policies in order to promote assimilation. Napoleon's consistorial system was of a piece with his policy of acknowledging and coopting Jewish leadership and institutions. He had called together the Assembly of Notables in 1806 to give an official and grandiose character to Jewish pledges of loyalty to state and society. Later, in 1807, he further solemnized the Jewish willingness to assimilate by convening a rabbinic body, the Grand Sanhedrin, which would ratify the decisions of the lay notables. Napoleon thereby deferred, at least obliquely, to the concept of rabbinic authority within the Jewish community. In the French case, as in the British one, Jewish interests and governmental interests in political modernization coincided and the new Jewish structures found state support.

The Alliance Israelite Universelle, founded in Paris in 1860, represents a different prototype. In this case, a Jewish organization was created not to assist government, but to lobby it. The persistence of anti-Semitism, the enduring and heightened sense of international Jewish mutuality and solidarity awakened by anti-Jewish outrages in Damascus and Bologna, motivated the French Jewish leadership. They wanted to create a voluntary, central body that could symbolically represent all Jews on a worldwide basis. Its practical work consisted of welfare activities among impoverished Jewries, development of schools in Palestine and elsewhere, as well as high-level political representation to the great powers. Although universal in conception and in name, in an age of nationalism, the Alliance could not shed its French particularity. Within several years, parallel organizations in England, Austria and Germany were created with similar goals.[6]

In the disappearance of the medieval autonomous community and its replacement by other forms of public body, we discern the political modernization of Jewish society against the background of gentile society's modernization. In general, modernization did not so much fundamentally negate as fundamentally transform the premodern structures.[7] Nonetheless, there are differences in the manner of transformation. In France, a revolutionary society oriented toward highly rational goals, the process of selection, appropriation and adaptation of communal institutions and practices was carried on with intensive state involvement. The resulting institutional pattern constituted a more deliberate break with the past than in England or Germany. In England, the transition toward Jewish political modernization was more gradual. In the conservative German states, by contrast, the transformation of Jewish institutions came about even more slowly than in England, albeit with significant governmental involvement as in France.

In Germany, the state governments saw their interests in the preservation of mandatory local communities and the inhibition of national, centralized bodies. The Prussian legislation of 1847 required that all Jews belong to, that is, pay taxes to support the religious, educational, and welfare activities of their local Jewish communities. The communities were empowered to elect their own officers according to their own procedures and to conduct their internal religious life as they saw fit. This legislation insured the quasi-official dominance of a traditional economic elite within the *Gemeinden*. By nature aristocratic, that is, nondemocratic, they were jealous of their privileges, suspicious of any attempt to create a supra-local institution, and passive vis-a-vis the conservative, hierarchical state. Thus German law and Jewish leadership atomized Prussian Jewry into over six hundred uncoordinated communities.[8] The situation was not fundamentally dissimilar in other German states. Although in Baden or Hesse consistory-like supervisory boards stood above the local communities, southern German Jewry was no less locally oriented than Prussian Jewry. Indeed, they were deeply suspicious of the north, a habit that impeded the growth of nationwide Orthodox organizations at the end of the century.

German governments took an active interest from the eighteenth through the late nineteenth century in maintaining the obligatory character of historic Jewish communal structures. Not until 1876, with the passage of the *Austrittsgesetz*, could a Jew resign from the local *Gemeinde* without having to renounce Judaism. Why should this be, given the extremity of German expectations of, indeed, demands for assimilation? On one level, the authorities considered the local communities to be useful providers of welfare services. In Frankfurt am

Main, for example, at the very moment of complete legal emancipation (1864), the city reassured its Christian citizens that Jews would still *have* to belong to the Jewish community and would not constitute a public burden on hospitals, schools or relief work.[9] The achievement of the right of secession from the *Gemeinde*, although ostensibly won in the name of freedom of religion, was part of a larger state policy during the Kulturkampf of eliminating the influence of traditional mediating structures, thereby enhancing the power of the centralized state. Thus the traditional framework of the *Gemeinde*, in its post-Emancipatory form, was retained by the state only to the extent that it served its purposes. By contrast, a nationwide organization, it was feared, would infringe on the paternal authority of the state. It would also represent too demonstrative an expression of a collective Jewish reality, thus, from both the Christian and the dominant Jewish points of view, impeding Jewish assimilation.[10]

Despite these difficulties, fledgling efforts toward creating a national organization began in 1869. The resulting *Deutsch-Israelitischer Gemeindebund* (German-Israelite Community Federation, DIGB) was, in fact, a union of local communities. It was primarily created in order to provide support for small rural communities through revenue sharing with the large urban centers. The migration to the cities during the period of industrialization constituted a problem for urban Jewries. Their attempts to reach out to rural Jews were not strictly altruistic.

Although the DIGB's initial mission was oriented toward educational and welfare concerns, the growing anti-Semitism of the 1870s oriented it toward defense work in the sense of public education and the representation of Jewish interests before the government. Rising anti-Semitism was probably the leading force making for solidarity among German Jews. Yet despite the clear need for such an organization, the DIGB foundered on the parochialism of the *Gemeinden* and lost heart before the adamancy of the anti-Semites and their supporters in government. The DIGB as a defense organization was effectively closed down by the Saxon government in 1881.

Its reorganized successor limited its focus to the original concern for intercommunity support.[11]

Governmental opposition, the lack, until 1871, of a unified nation state and strong traditions of localism combined to frustrate mass Jewish organization in Germany. An additional factor was German Jewry's powerful intellectual and practical commitment to political liberalism. The liberal parties were the political home of most German Jews in the nineteenth century. Their leaders lent support to the Jewish striving for equality, less out of philosemitism than out of their own commitment to the ideal of a state governed by the principle of equality under the law *(Rechtsstaat)*.[12] Liberalism was the intellectual credo of assimilationism. Intellectually, the liberal conception of the world was more or less incompatible with claims to a specifically Jewish national existence. One stood before the state as a citizen, not as a Jew. This worldview could not intially conceive of the endurance of a collective Jewish problem. Given the attainment of statutory legal equality by the mid- and late-1860s, a Jewish problem ought not to have existed. Individual Jews might continue to experience problems of discrimination, but the Jews as a whole were now simply citizens. Like other citizens, should they suffer discrimination, they could sue for redress of grievances in the courts. If the political and judicial institutions were insufficiently responsive it was not because they targeted Jews in some invidious way, it was because the *Rechtsstaat* had not yet triumphed over the inertia and arbitrariness of the bureaucracy. The problem was the achievement of a fully responsive *Rechtsstaat*. Thus the liberal forces, Jewish and German, which brought about legal emancipation, trusted in the evolving *Rechtsstaat* to solve any lingering impediments to successful integration. This perspective saw no need for intermediary Jewish political agencies. They could only signify a giant step backward toward medieval segregation and separatism. Indeed, the persistent demands of German political liberals, as well as Christian theological liberals, that nonbelieving Jews ought to shed their remaining, now unjustified distinctiveness, and become Christian indicates a fundamental hostility toward Jewish community per se.

The shift away from faith in a dawning liberal society to a renewed reliance on particularistic, Jewish political action took place in the 1870s–1890s in confrontation with the rise of modern, political anti-Semitism. The dawn of a new age brought a culture of illiberalism. Precisely at the time when full legal equality was achieved, the liberal interpretation of reality was subverted by German society's reluctance to accept the Jews as social equals. For decades, Jews had operated on the assumption that a radical and thoroughgoing assimilation would cement their emancipation and facilitate their integration. The demand for a total transformation of Jewishness, indeed the expectation of its total disappearance, was stronger in Germany than elsewhere, for Germany had its own unique problem of unification and nation building.[13] Nationalism's profound spiritual dimension: salvation through complete identification with the national spirit, could not tolerate the dissonance of a large, national minority. Yet, by the last decades of the century, the criteria of *Deutschtum* had changed. With anti-Semitism, racial or at least ethnic categories acquired symbolic dominance. Insofar as the Jew cannot escape his "race," assimilation is neither possible nor desirable. Crude opinions of this sort, promoted by anti-Semitic propagandists and politicians, had their sophisticated counterparts and made alarming progress in elite sectors of the society such as the professoriate. Jewish contemporaries strove to explain the gap between statutory equality and social reality as an understandable cultural lag.[14] But while the electoral success of the anti-Semitic parties waned by the mid-1880s (only to rise impressively in the 1890s), their views did not lose their currency. Anti-Semitism in its modern racialist form became a pervasive dimension of German politics and cultural life. However one chose to explain it, it became undeniable that there remained a collective Jewish problem, not just a problem of distinct, Jewish individuals. Discrimination was systemic, not merely episodic. This factor called German Jews back to the commonality of their condition.

The traditional German Jewish leadership, the heads of the large *Gemeinden*, had earlier frustrated the formation of an effective DIGB. While they were certainly aware of growing anti-Semitism and systemic discrimination against Jews, they were ill-equipped to deal with it. They knew from decades of experience that public prosecutors (who held a monopoly on what cases could be brought to court with the State's presumptive approval) were indifferent toward Jewish claims of discrimination. The administrative bureaucracy was unwilling to enforce its own standards of fairness. The old line leadership's attitude was one of resignation. They feared that vigorous activism would only stir up more anti-Semitism. Anti-Semites accused Jews of being domineering and arrogant. Publically visible protest would only cement this image in the public mind. The DIGB, after some initial legal challenges to anti-Semitic agitators and pamphlets, assumed the same posture of resignation, contenting itself with publishing popular-scholarly, apologetic presentations about Judaism. In addition, although anti-Semitism was hateful and crude, the highly assimilated leadership implicitly agreed with some of its charges. Jews had not become German enough. They still had their own physical features, body language, habits of mind. There were always immigrant Ostjuden who fulfilled the cultural stereotypes and embarassed the German Jews before their fellow citizens. Indeed, the Orthodox, despite their substantial assimilation to Germanness, were often pilloried by the old line community leadership as an embarassing relic of medieval seperatism.

In 1891–92, a ritual murder accusation against a kosher slaughterer and his family in Xanten outraged the German Jewish community. The Board of the Berlin community secretly prepared a letter to the Emperor begging for his protection against anti-Semitism. The existence of the petition became public knowledge and the Board, embarassed, opted not to send it. Even more than its inaction, the posture of special pleading, of appearing like medieval *Schutzjuden* (protected Jews), angered the younger members of the community. It was undignified to ask the Emperor for favors. The appropriate stance for the Jews was to confidently assert and proudly defend their rights.[15] Having come of age after the achievement of emancipation, this younger generation of German Jews had a confidence as both Jews and Germans which enabled them to move beyond the creed-like pieties of liberal assimilationism. In response to this widespread sentiment among the younger leadership that Jewish dignity required assertive, Jewish action, two hundred Jews met in Berlin in 1893 and founded what was to become the most influential German Jewish mass organization, the *Centralverein deutscher Staatsbürger jüdischen Glaubens* (CV).[16]

Unlike the DIGB, the CV's purpose was explicitly political, albeit nonpartisan. Although not intended to be a Jewish party—that option was rejected by most from the start—it was intended to be a force for public education and public pressure in the defense of Jewish rights. Moreover, it took an active role in electoral campaigns, urging Jewish voters to support candidates who were not anti-Semites or who opposed anti-Semitism. It also supported candidates with financial contributions. The CV took shape at a time when many groups in German society, for example, Junkers, farmers, Catholics, and others formed lobbies (*Interessenverbände*) to advance their interests, often by exchanging the votes of their constituencies for political favors.[17] On this level, it was a Jewish *Interessenverband*.

At another level, the CV signaled a quiet revolution in Jewish identity and consciousness.[18] It sought to capture the symbolic center of German Jewish life and create a new discourse of Jewish identity in the context of German nationality. This discourse deepened the meaning of Jewishness. Its educational work among Jews increasingly stressed sound knowledge of Jewish history and sources as the foundation of identity and pride. It eschewed self-hate and refused to endorse any of the stock criticisms against Jewish character which even relatively sympathetic Christians like the leaders of the *Verein zur Abwehr des Antisemitismus* espoused. To be sure, it worked out its strengthened Jewishness within the parameters of German citizenship and *Deutschtum*. Its philosophy remained liberal in the sense that it conceived of its task as one of making Germany an enlightened, prejudice-free country where social life corresponded to legal norms. But it did glimpse an horizon beyond mere assimilationism: pride, knowledge, historical consciousness, self-help were the marks of its new Jewishness.

Orthodox Jews responded to this half-century of organizational creativity with ambivalence. The community of Samson Raphael Hirsch, firmly anchored in a posture of noncooperation with liberal Jews, distanced itself from both the DIGB and the CV. The DIGB, as a union of compulsory communities, stood precisely for the institution the Hirschians were trying to overthrow: the state-sponsored, obligatory community. The Hirschians and the DIGB clashed repeatedly, particularly over efforts to unite all of Prussian Jewry in a single, state-recognized consistorial body.[19] The CV, more intent on being a true mass organization, was far more solicitous of Orthodox needs and sensitivities, often against the wishes of its Reform membership and leadership. This could not suffice to coopt southern German orthodoxy. It disparaged not only the CV's liberal conception, but also held its primary function, fighting anti-Semitism, to be futile. Anti-Semitism was a dispensation of Providence, given to bring assimilated German Jews back to tradition. Northern German Orthodoxy, typified by the pragmatic traditionalism of Esriel Hildesheimer and the Rabbiner Seminar in Berlin, by contrast, took a more cooperative, if not always enthusiastic stance.[20]

Nonetheless, the pressures toward centralized organization also played upon the Orthodox community. In a development that paralleled the creation of the DIGB, the Hirsch community formed the *Freie Vereinigung für die Interessen des orthodoxen Judentums* in 1886. This organization increasingly came to assume the full range of functions carried out by the CV, indeed by international organizations such as the Alliance and its German counterpart, the *Hilfsverein der deutschen Juden* (1901). As the *Freie Vereinigung* (FV), by Jacob Rosenheim's own admission, was the "seed" of Agudat Israel, we must attend to its self-conception, activity and structure.

ORTHODOXY IN AN AGE OF ORGANIZATION:
THE FREIE VEREINIGUNG FÜR DIE INTERESSEN
DES ORTHODOXEN JUDENTUMS

Samson Raphael Hirsch called, in September 1885, for
the creation of an organization to take up the collective tasks
of German Orthodox Jewry.[21] In the first sentence of Hirsch's
summons, he characteristically combined an appeal to
medieval tradition with his own modernist-Orthodox tendency:

> The spirit of association, of *haverut*, of the voluntary
> union of the like-minded for common purposes, which
> is so prominent today, was and is alive and well, in Jewish
> circles, especially for the purposes of spiritual and ethical
> improvement (*Bildung*) and for the well-meaning love of
> man, since time immemorial.[22]

Hirsch paired the voluntaristic, practical spirit of the age
with the classical Jewish will to polity, orienting both to his
Enlightenment-inspired philosophy of *Bildung*. He offered a
brief, romantic precis of the *havurah* of old. Not a mere task-
oriented society, the *havurah* was a solemn assembly, its
members bound together by oath to seek the highest plane of
mutual responsibility and consciousness of Jewish duty. The
ancient and archetypal *haver*-institution was the most effective factor in the transmission of Jewish knowledge and law.
Hirsch was evidently making reference to the society of sages
within pharisaic-tannaitic Judaism, thereby reaching back to
the most authoritative historical precedents for his idea.[23]
Hirsch opined that this great communal legacy was still
latent among the Orthodox and asserts that the time was right
for its reinstantiation. Only through a large, voluntary organization could welfare, cultural and educational needs, as well as
the need to represent Orthodox Jewry before the state authorities be met.[24]
The tasks of the new organization would parallel those of
the DIGB. First, the organization would need to promote

authentic Jewish and authentic general education (*Bildung*) through creating and financing schools of various types, including yeshivot, and supporting teachers and those who wish to become teachers. Second, the FV must stimulate the development of reliable services for orthodox travellers such as hotels and restaurants. An important dimension of this would be assisting in creating or maintaining proper ritual baths and kosher slaughterhouses. Hirsch was particularly concerned with the preservation of Orthodox institutions in small towns. Like the DIGB initiative, the FV envisioned support of rural communities, increasingly impoverished by emigration, to be a key element of its mission.

Hirsch listed among the organization's projected goals measures to alleviate the pressures of employment on Orthodox youth, such as a job listing service for positions where observance would not be a hinderance to employment and an unemployment security insurance fund. Serving the needs of Orthodox soldiers and prisoners was also considered.

While Hirsch was concerned to publicize the "inalienable fundamental laws" of Jewish communal life in order to advise communities on the rights and duties of their boards and members, he also explicitly foreswore intervention into local matters, (a course later followed by Agudah). Hirsch, perhaps the most dedicated exponent of communal autonomy in Germany, did not envision the creation of a consistorial body with supervisory powers over individual communities. Indeed, attempts on the liberal side to create such a body were vigorously opposed by separatist Orthodoxy. The separatists feared that the overwhelming preponderance of Reform Jews would dominate any such body and nullify their right to exist.[25]

Nonetheless, Hirsch did believe that the inauguration of a free union of Orthodox Jews would constitute *the* authoritative Jewish public body, that is, the true representative of authentic Judaism in German. The FV would act, as had the DIGB, to explain and defend Judaism before state and society. But the FV would explain and defend the *real* Judaism, the only Judaism worth living and fighting for. He concluded his call with a prophetic quotation (Malachi 3:16–17) reminding

Israel that while the many have apostasized and will be judged, the few are the true sons of God. Even though the Orthodox are the numerical minority, they are the remnant of Israel who fear God's name and are His treasured people (segulah).

Hirsch's argument is an artful piece of conservative thought. While essentially rational and practical, it appeals to both Jewish historical precedent (the havurah) and to divine sanction, that is, prophetic instruction (the necessity for the minority of true believers to represent the wayward majority of backsliders) for legitimation.[26] Here we see the near seamless combination of the rational and the mythic, the Enlightenment liberalism and the romantic conservativism that marks his and other German Orthodox discourse. Rosenheim's synthesis of tradition and modernity is firmly anchored in this Hirschian style of thinking.

Following Hirsch's summons, the FV was organized the following year. In the period between Hirsch's death (1888) and its reorganization under Jacob Rosenheim in 1906, the FV engaged in the wide spectrum of activities outlined in Hirsch's initial proposal. It was extensively involved in supporting Orthodox students, teachers, ritual circumcisors, as well as in promoting uniform standards of circumcision and kashrut. Its defense and propaganda work included commissioning expert opinions from Christian academics on the humanity of kosher slaughter and lobbying Reichstag members to keep such slaughter legal.[27]

Constitutionally, the organization had a mass membership of Jews who professed the tenets of Orthodoxy. It sought like-minded Jews (Gesinnungsgenossen) of unimpeachable character (unbescholtene Jude) and did not discriminate between those who belonged to mixed communities and those who belonged to separatist communities.[28] Despite initial expectations that the FV might become the common address for all Orthodox Jews, however, the organization remained largely a Frankfurt, separatist affair, with a low membership. Efforts to expand its base in the north, as we shall see, foundered on the strict separatist ideology of Hirsch's successor, Salomon Breuer. This same tension between "church" and "sect," that is, between the goals of Orthodox inclusivity and Orthodox organizational purity, were to mark the history of Agudat Israel as well. In the case of both organizations there was a struggle over the ideal orientation of the group. Should the group be guided by essentially pragmatic, instrumentally rational, that is, political values or should the group stand and fall on those transcendent values (*Wertrationalität*) which ultimately validate it? How political can the group afford to be and still symbolically represent Torah-true Jewry as its polity?

The members of the FV had to pay a modest charge of three marks per year. The membership, which met every three years, elected a board of twenty to twenty-five members, which met at least once per year. This board in turn elected a five to seven member executive committee out of its own ranks which ran the organization.[29] This three tiered structure mirrors, to a certain extent, the constitution of the old Frankfurt *kehillah*, discussed above.[30] A commission of rabbis advised the executive committee, insuring the conformity of their decisions with established halakhic guidelines. As in the communal constitutions, the rabbinate was a creature of the lay board, deriving its function and authority from the communal leadership.[31] The board, however, voluntarily consented to the advice and counsel of the rabbinate. In theory, agreement on fundamental principles would harmonize the potentially dissonant perspectives of the lay leaders (similar to the medieval *Vorsteher* or *ba'alei ha-takkanot*) and the rabbis. In practice, these distinctions were blurred. For many years, the president of the FV, Rabbi Breuer, was also the head of its rabbinical commission, the *keter Torah* and the *keter malchut*, to use Daniel Elazar's terminology, were united in the same individual.[32] Furthermore, the relations between Rabbi Breuer and the lay board, led by Jacob Rosenheim from 1906 on, were anything but harmonious. Indeed, the disharmony began at the level of fundamental principle. At any rate, this basic design, with its evocative, historical allusions to the medieval *kehillah*, served as the model for Agudat Israel as well.

Naphtali Hirsch, the executive director of the FV died in 1905. At the beginning of 1906, Jacob Rosenheim was chosen by the board of directors to be the executive. He accepted only on condition that he could reorganize the FV into a more comprehensive and representative body. He aspired, that is, to unite all of German Orthodoxy under the wings of an expanded Freie Vereinigung. Should he fail in this task, he indicated, he would resign.[33]

German Orthodoxy was ideologically fragmented, as we have noted, between the separatists (members of seven so-called *Austrittsgemeinden*), on the Frankfurt model, and those Orthodox who were accomodated within the historic community after a separatist group formed (*Gemeindeorthodox*). In addition, many Orthodox Jews lived in unified historic communities (*Einheitsgemeinden*) which had never experienced a split.[34] In some, for example, Halberstadt, the Orthodox dominated the *Gemeinde*. Even though an *Austrittsgemeinde* existed in Berlin, its leadership and tradition were oriented toward practical cooperation with other Jewish groups. Indeed, the graduates of Esriel Hildesheimer's rabbinical seminary often served congregations in mixed communities. A distinguished graduate, Rabbi Marcus Horowitz, became the rabbi of the *Gemeindeorthodox* ("Börneplatz") synagogue in Frankfurt, a fact that was to cause enduring dissension in Orthodox ranks. Ultimately, no separatist community was more committed to separatism as a religious principle than Frankfurt. Thus the fissure within Orthodoxy was not only along communal lines, but also along geographic lines. The south (e.g., Frankfurt, Wiesbaden, Darmstadt) was more adamant about noncooperation with *Gemeindeorthodoxie* than the separatist communities of the north.

Rosenheim was convinced that a union of Orthodox Jews from every stream was absolutely necessary. He believed that what Orthodox Jews had in common was more significant than what separated them. The immediate impetus toward an Orthodox union was a repeated attempt at creating a general union of German Jewry in the early 1900s.[35] Another ritual murder accusation in 1900 galvanized the leadership and supporters of the CV to work to create a comprehensive, consistorial system which could provide authoritative representation for German Jewry vis-a-vis the government. The belief always was that a government-accredited central agency would raise the dignity and credibility of Judaism in Germany and thus prove a more effective antidote to anti-Semitism and bureaucratic inertia, not to mention hostility, than the currently fragmented communities and voluntaristic defense organizations. This proposal met with Orthodox support from leaders of the *Gemeindeorthodox* and *Einheitsgemeinde* streams. Accordingly, Rosenheim and other separatist leaders felt it imperative to win the non-separatists back from this movement and to create their own pan-Orthodox union.

At stake for Rosenheim was not only the defense of *Austrittsgemeinden*, but the survival of Orthodoxy as a movement of principles. Rosenheim contended that anti-Semitism put an end to earlier liberal illusions of boundless assimilation. Jews were forced back to a renewed sense of collective destiny by collective marginalisation. While tradition took on renewed sacredness for some, welfare, cultural, and organizational activity became the functional religion of many.[36] While not inherently deplorable, however, this return to the roots movement was based on ethnicity and sentimentality, not on the hard bedrock of the Jewish polity, that is, the Torah. Accordingly, Rosenheim felt that it was essential to bring Orthodoxy back to the true ground of its existence, belief in the divine character of Torah, and to craft its organizational unity on this principle. Otherwise, Orthodoxy would come to see itself as merely the traditional stream of a Jewry self-defined by ties of blood and sentiment, rather than by religious principle.

This rationalized, formative principle of Orthodoxy was "torah min shamayim," Torah from heaven:

> concerning the divinely revealed and continuing, binding character of the written and oral law, no difference of opinion arises between the various directions within Torah-loyal (*gesetztreuen*) Judaism. Over and against this indubitable, principled basis of organized cooperation,

the remaining differences are controversies of second rank, perhaps only tactical matters of no significant weight.[37]

Like Hirsch, Rosenheim returns to a clear belief in the divinity and ideal-regulative nature of the Torah as the bedrock of Orthodoxy, indeed, of Judaism. This stress on an idea per se, a rationalized, articulated principle as the basis of present collective life and as the ideal for future organization characterizes his enterprise as what we earlier called, following Karl Mannheim, liberal-humanitarian utopianism.[38] In this utopian framework, a system of ideas, believed to both fit social reality and to be in some way inherent within it, serves as the regulative, normative model for social evolution. Rosenheim had to bring Orthodox public reality into conformity with its inherent/ideal nature.[39] He had to forge a new social consensus on the basis of a return to constitutional first principles. To recall our earlier formulation, the true Jewish polity had to be won back from the debased and disenchanted empirical community to which it had deteriorated. It, as well as the Jews, had to be restored through a renewal of the Torah-constitution.

The goal of union based on mutual recognition of a shared idea made considerable progress under Rosenheim's leadership in 1907. Empowered by Rabbi Breuer and the FV's leadership, he conducted negotiations in the first half of the year with leaders of northern German Orthodoxy and the circle around the rabbinical seminary in Berlin. The personal contacts of friends and relatives, as well as Rosenheim's own considerable skills as a mediator, smoothed over difficulties caused by many years of tension and estrangement.[40] Bouyed by support in the north, the FV held a meeting in June, 1907, at which it revised its constitution and expanded its board to include representatives of northern German Orthodoxy. The seven member executive committee was expanded to thirteen members, with northerners holding key posts on both the committee and the board. Jacob Rosenheim and Benjamin Hirsch of Halberstadt shared the vice-presidency under Rabbi Breuer.

Although Rosenheim succeeded in laying a basis for a broad Orthodox union, complete inclusiveness escaped him. Breuer's unbridgeable differences with Marcus Horowitz, finally excluded Frankfurt *Gemeindeorthodoxie* from the FV.[41] Breuer would allow no common ground with Horowitz. In his view, the continued existence of the *Religionsgesellschaft* was based on a fundamental denial of communal orthodoxy's right to exist. This denial was institutionalized as a boycott of or, in Rosenheim's term, a *herem* (i.e., ban) against, the Börneplatz synagogue and its rabbi.[42]

Rabbi Salomon Breuer, no less than Rosenheim, was a man of ideas. In his view (as represented by his son, Isaac Breuer), what divides the Orthodox is more significant than what unites them. What divides them are fundamentally discrepant concepts of community. Community (*Gemeinschaftsleben*) is the fundamental Jewish reality, the recipient and custodian of the divine Torah on earth. The collectivity has its own integral existence. It is not a union of individuals. It transcends its individuals. To find a commonality of belief (which does, as a matter of empirical fact, exist) with the *Gemeindeorthodox* is beside the point. The issue is not what individuals can agree on. It is the objective legitimacy of the collective Israel, of the *kehillat Yaacov*, that they claim to represent.[43] *Gemeindeorthodoxie*, by its very existence, betrays the Torah because it implies that Orthodoxy is a preference alongside other preferences or opinions about Judaism. Its willingness, as a matter of institutional fact, to legitimate its Reform partner in the *Gemeinde* disqualifies it from representing *kehillat Yaacov* in Frankfurt. *Gemeindeorthodoxie* represents a group of Jews with traditional beliefs and practices. The *Religionsgesellschaft*, by contrast, represents the eternal Israel.

Breuer's intense opposition, which would also complicate the creation and early career of Agudat Israel, was based on an idea no less than was Rosenheim's. Both had a highly rationalized, that is idea-oriented construction of Judaism. One can not say that Rosenheim was pragmatic and Breuer was ideological, that Rosenheim subordinated ideas to practice more than Breuer. Both oriented their action toward ideas (i.e., engaged in *wertrational* action). Breuer's idea was to take the organic, essentialistic model of sacral peoplehood to its limit. Israel is wholly one with its law. Rosenheim, while not rejecting this idea, gave more latitude to the consensual/covenantal pole of Jewish self-representation.

Another way of looking at this is to say that they assessed the social situation of Orthodoxy differently because they had different fundamental understandings of the relationship of the sacred and the profane. Breuer believed everything depended upon an intact sacred center, an halakhically legitimated and administered, reified collectivity. He typified the "administrative" tendency toward social action and denied to politics its sphere of instrumental, rationally-oriented action. Breuer also, not surprisingly, insisted on a high degree of rabbinic involvement and oversight of policy making.

Rosenheim, by contrast, believed that the center needed the periphery and would collapse without it. The periphery is, by definition of course, less sacred than the center. Rosenheim needed to extend the sacredness of the center into the periphery. While Breuer wanted to preserve the center from any diminution of its sacredness, Rosenheim was willing to take risks for the sake of the sacred or at least to take a different kind of risk. (Breuer was willing to wager his own credibility because of his "hardline" stance.) Rosenheim was more willing than Breuer to risk the threat of disenchantment. Rosenheim was the more political man. He had a higher threshhold of tolerance for the disenchanting, desacralizing aspects of political life.[44]

Rosenheim tried to preserve the sacred by constantly relating political, that is, instrumentally rational action to an ethically rational, that is, *wertrational* schema of ideas and values. The periphery must constantly be reclaimed by the center. Breuer, by contrast, although intellectually persuaded of the necessity of broadened, communal activity, could not square this policy with his deepest convictions about the way the sacred endures in the world. The sacred requires archetypal purity, isolation. He rejected politics in the sense of risk-taking, instrumental action. It was too far removed from the bedrock of *Wertrationalität*. If a course of action could not be explicitly legitimated by clear halakhic principle, in this case Hirsch's judgment on the ineluctability of separatism and its perceived consequences, then it must be rejected as too profane. Thus Breuer opted away from politics for the sake of sacred administration. We will consider the consequences of this option for Agudat Israel below.

The expanded, reorganized FV met in Berlin in December 1907. Its ongoing work was divided between several committees including: Propaganda, Legislation and Administration; Literature and the Press; Education; Religious Affairs; Eastern European Jewry, as well as a commission for the Land of Israel (*Palästina Kommission*).[45] This latter commission was, by Jacob Rosenheim's own testimony, the kernal out of which Agudat Israel developed.

The FV became involved in "Erez Jisroel Arbeit" (Palestine colonization and welfare work) through several channels. The first was the traditional cooperative arrangement between the Dutch and German Orthodox in support of the Ashkenazi traditional community in Jerusalem. In 1809, a family of Orthodox Dutch bankers, the Lehren's, established a society of *"Pekidim* and *Amarkalim* for the Holy Land" called *Kolel Hod* (= an abbreviation for "Holland v'Deutschland") to coordinate fundraising activities in western Europe. The organization was based in Amsterdam, but drew heavily on German funds. Rabbis of several German cities, along with Dutch Jews, constituted its board. By 1906, Rabbi Breuer, convinced that there was insufficient oversight and direction, refused to endorse the traditional procedure. Rosenheim, at Breuer's behest, convened a conference at which the FV took over the entire operation and initiated a modern, policy-driven welfare system with a full-time employee in Jerusalem.[46] This required delicate negotiations with the traditional Ashkenazi rabbinate in Jerusalem, which needed to be convinced that a departure from the customary disbursement of funds to needy families was justified. At any rate, this involvement was the opening wedge for closer contacts between German Orthodoxy and the changing society of Jewish Palestine.

But concern for modern administration, oversight, and accountability was not the only reason that the FV expanded its support of the Old Yishuv. Rosenheim was particularly concerned about the growth of secular, Zionist-oriented activity both there and in Germany. Secular Zionism did not pose a direct threat to Western Orthodoxy. The *Zionistische Vereinigung für Deutschland* (1897) drew its membership from the same relatively assimilated circles as the CV. At the same time, the Orthodox component of the Zionist movement, Mizrachi, did offer some competition even within the Frankfurt separatist community, but remained a minority option. Zionism did, however, pose an ideological challenge and an aggressive, new competition on the ground, as it were, in the Land of Israel. The FV sought to stem the nascent secularist influence in Palestine by planning and funding religious schools in the new Jewish colonies.[47]

The ideological challenge posed by Zionism was in Herzl's conception of the Zionist movement as the historical agent/savior (*gestor negotiorum*) of the Jewish people. In *The Jewish State*, Herzl wrote:

> The Romans, with their marvellous sense of justice, produced that noble masterpiece, the *negotiorum gestio*. When the property of an oppressed person is in danger, any man may step forward to save it. This man is the *gestor*, the director of affairs not strictly his own. He has received no warrant—that is, no human warrant; higher obligations authorize him to act . . . The *gestio* is intended to work for the good of the *dominus*—the people, to whom the *gestio* himself belongs.[48]

Herzl devised this ingenious theory, on the basis of Roman legal concepts, to authorize his movement to act on behalf of the entire people. Despite the fact that Herzl's political Zionists represented the barest minority of Jews, they represented themselves as the agents of *klal Israel*: Zionist institutions, such as the Congresses, were presented as a parliament for the entire polity.[49]

Herzlian Zionism was profoundly threatening to confessionalized Western Jewry due to its outright espousal of the
national and political character of Judaism. The German
Orthodox, for all their efforts at confessionalization, however,
retained more of a sense of peoplehood, of metahistorical, collective existence than their Reform brethren. They also, for
the most part, rejected Herzl, but not necessarily because he
threatened their *Deutschtum*. Rather, his strictly secular
nationalism offended against the religiously informed sense of
national identity and, furthermore, of political identity which
they continued, perhaps half-unconsciously, to nurture. They
did not require an ingenious borrowing from Roman jurispru-
dence in order to see their own group as the saving remnant.
Their sense of being the last, loyal core of Israel and of acting
on Israel's behalf in history antedates, as we have seen, Herzl's
activity. Nonetheless, it is undeniable that Herzlian Zionism
stirred up the potential for greater self-reflection, conceptual
refinement and indeed, political activism, among the Frankfurt
circle. Political Zionism challenged them to represent themselves in more overtly national and political categories as the
"gestor negotiorum" of God's *'am segulah*.

The FV, therefore, was to become more involved in prac-
tical work in Palestine. The leading force behind enhancing
Rosenheim's and the FV's involvement was the historian,
Rabbi Isaac Itzig Halevy (1847–1914).[50] Halevy, a master of
rabbinic literature and author of a quasi-modernist history of
the halakha, settled in Germany after fleeing his native
Lithuania. From 1902 on, he served as the "Klaus Rabbi" in
Hamburg, spending his summers in Bad Homburg near
Frankfurt. His close friendships, formed in childhood, with
the leading scholars of Lithuania would later form the bridge
to the East needed to build Agudat Israel. He also maintained
close relations with a number of German rabbis, including R.
Marcus Horowitz, the communal Orthodox rabbi in Frankfurt,
and with Rabbi Abraham Isaac Kook, the emerging leader of
the Ashkenazi community in Palestine.

In 1907, Halevy was invited to join the publication commission of the FV, which had earlier helped to sponsor his his-

torical research. Eager to expand his sphere of activity, he also asked to join the Palestine committee, headed by Rosenheim, as Jewish education in Palestine was one of his major concerns.[51] Halevy believed from the outset that the Palestine committee of the FV should broaden its scope and become an effective international agency. From his correspondence, it is clear that he believed that Orthodox institutions should compete with entities such as the World Zionist Organization.[52] Halevy, though an arch traditionalist and inclined toward separatism, did not make separatism a pillar of his philosophy. In addition to his friendship with Marcus Horowitz, he urged cooperation with the network of German schools ("Ezra") in Palestine maintained by the *Hilfsverein der Deutschen Juden*, if Orthodox conditions could be met. He urged, as well, that the language of the land, Arabic or Turkish, be taught to children in the religious schools. It is possible that, as an outsider, Halevy was naturally inclined to work beyond the borders of Germany and to transcend German Orthodoxy's ideological and cultural boundaries. The leavening role of the cultural outsider was perhaps Halevy's greatest contribution. Halevy's combination of openness to innovation, pragmatism, and organizational ability made him a highly effective, credible leader.

The picture that emerges from Halevy's letters is that he was the true originator of the Agudah idea. On his own testimony, he pushed for expanding the role of the Palestine committee to become an inclusive, Orthodox representation for colonization work, the building of schools and the development of a cultural and religious infrastructure. In Halevy's letter to his friend, the Bad Homburg rabbi, R. Kottek, in November, 1908, he relates how he tried to convince Rosenheim to develop the FV in this direction. He says that he proposed the name "Agudat Israel" to Rosenheim for this new, comprehensive, independent agency.[53]

Rosenheim's reaction was hesitant. Rosenheim, as well as R. Salomon Breuer, feared that the organization proposed by Halevy was too "Palestinocentric," that is, too similar to Zionism in conception. They believed that a more effective approach to Palestine was required, but that this could occur within the framework of the FV. Halevy argued that a truly effective organization must transcend the limits of German Jewry. Indeed, Rosenheim and Breuer wanted cooperation with Eastern European Jewry. Their anxiety about appearing "too Zionist" was in part inspired by their desire not to alienate the East.[54]

Rosenheim summed up the implication of these deliberations in an address to the annual meeting (Vereinstag) of the FV in December, 1908. The Orthodox minority in Germany must find a way of making common cause with the Orthodox masses in the East. The two Jewries need each other. Rosenheim appears to have worked out a compromise position with Halevy. A new organization would be created, embracing both Western and Eastern European Jews. Its work would include, but not be restricted to, Palestine concerns. As we shall see, the proper role of Palestine in the agenda of Agudat Israel remained a contested point.[55]

AGUDAT ISRAEL

The decision of the FV to create a comprehensive, international organization led to a conference in August, 1909, in Bad Homburg, a spa near to Frankfurt, where Halevy and other eastern rabbis and laymen were accustomed to spend their summers. The eastern leaders included both mitnaggdim such as R. Chaim Soloveitchik of Brisk, R. Eliezer Rabbinowitz of Minsk, R. Eliezer Gordon of Telz, R. Chaim Ozer Grodzenski of Vilna, as well as hasidim such as the rabbi of Gur, R. Mordechai Alter, and a representative of the Lubavitcher Rebbe. Hungarian Orthodoxy was represented by Adolf Frankel, the president of the federation of Hungarian Orthodox communities.[56] The fact that R. Marcus Horowitz could not be invited continued to disturb Rosenheim. Halevy worked behind the scenes to pacify Horowitz and to reassure Rosenheim.

While Halevy was personally friendly with and highly respectful toward R. Horowitz, he also did not think that Horowitz was philosophically sympathetic to Agudah. Halevy explained to Rosenheim that Horowitz and his followers view the Orthodox as a group of traditional individuals who have banded together in a contractual manner to secure their way of life. They see themselves not as *klal Israel* per se, but as a traditionalist minority. The Agudah conception, on the contrary, understands the Orthodox as *klal Israel* per se, demographic statistics notwithstanding. The Agudist conception, as articulated by Halevy, and certainly shared by Rosenheim and Breuer, is what we have termed organic and essentialistic. Horowitz's conception is contingent and contractarian.[57]

Two controversial issues emerged in this meeting which would continue to play a major role in Agudah's early history. The first was the Breuer/Hungarian insistence on the necessity for and preeminence of separatist orthodoxy wherever it existed. The second was the reluctance of the eastern rabbis to give Palestinian concerns too much centrality.

In response to the first concern, the conferees established the principle of local autonomy. The new organization would not mix into the affairs of a community or country without approval of the local rabbinate. The Agudah, in other words, would not become an hierarchical institution, but would assume a federal form.[58] The federal orientation constitutes one strong and unmistakable link with the historic Jewish political tradition. As we noted above, the super-*kehillah* organizations of the middle ages, including the Frankfurt synod of 1603, insisted on preserving local autonomy. Ironically, the Breuer/Hungarian faction which promoted this orientation was the first to violate it. Its eventual demand that only members of separatist communities, in areas where such communities existed, were fit to serve in leadership positions was a clear violation of its own insistence on deference to local conditions. Another consequence of this federal orientation was that Eastern European Jewry would be given leadership roles in the future organization in proportion to its numerical weight.

The Russian rabbis wanted to proclaim the founding of Agudat Israel immediately, but the Germans insisted on waiting until the next plenary meeting of the FV. The conferees contented themselves with requesting that the board and executive committee of the FV create a provisional committee in Frankfurt to lay the financial, organizational and constitutional groundwork for an orthodox world congress.[59]

The board of the FV, conscious of the great historical importance of the proposal, approved this request in February 1910.[60] Over the next year and one-half, however, internal discord led to a sense of exhaustion and a near abandonment of the project. The absolute refusal of R. Breuer to include R. Horowitz and the Frankfurt Gemeindeorthodox in the deliberations created enormous tension between Breuer and the head of the provisional committee, Louis Feist. Feist, the President of the IRG as such, was also a paying member of the *Gemeinde* and a friend of Horowitz's. Feist insisted that if R. Horowitz could not be on the provisional committee, then no other rabbi could be on it either. Accordingly, the Western rabbinate had no representative, and rabbinic guidance came from the east, a fact that greatly annoyed R. Breuer.[61]

In addition to the local difficulties in Frankfurt, a worsening political situation in Russia complicated correspondence with the eastern rabbis. According to Rosenheim, work on Agudah came to a virtual dead end in 1910, although Halevy's letters present a somewhat different picture. Halevy remained active, perhaps on his own, in designing the Agudah. He proposed a model constitution in 1910 which gave expression to his highly essentialistic, organic understanding of Jewish peoplehood.[62] Halevy's draft speaks of Agudat Israel as the unification of all Jews who obey Torah and mitsvot in all the diasporas and in Israel. These Jews represent and speak for the whole nation (*ha-oomah b'khlalah*). All must cooperate to strengthen Torah education, especially in Israel and in America; to better the living conditions of impoverished Jews; and to promote true knowledge of Torah and of Jewish history, that is, to combat the spread of alien forms of Wissenschaft.[63] These concerns, although with a somewhat different emphasis, would later be adopted in the statutes of Agudat Israel.

The efforts to develop an organization might have collapsed were it not for an eventful coincidence. The 10th Zionist Congress, meeting in Basel in August 1911, endorsed a platform of cultural work in the diaspora, against the wishes of its Mizrachi minority. Although cultural work, such as supporting the renaissance of the Hebrew language, developing educational materials and institutions with a secular-nationalist orientation and so on, had never been absent from Zionism's agenda, the movement as a whole downplayed culture as a potentially divisive force and was focused, at least at the highest level, on political negotiation. By 1911, however, frustration with the lack of political progress gave the practical Zionists, that is, advocates of piecemeal colonization and diaspora consciousness-raising and political organizing (*Gegenwartsarbeit*) the upper hand. As the leadership swung from its initial Herzlian legacy to practical work, the cultural component was included in the movement's resolutions.[64] The Mizrachi, whose participation in the Zionist Organization was contingent on it maintaining its strictly pragmatic, political character were bitterly disappointed by this endorsement of an ideological stance that frontally challenged traditional Judaism. Rabbi Arthur Cohn of Basel called, in the pages of the *Israelit*, for the Mizrachi federation as such to separate itself from the Zionist Organization and to join the efforts to create a pan-Orthodox representation. Although the Mizrachi delegates did walk out of the hall, Mizrachi as a whole decided subsequently to remain in the ZO. At this point, four of its leading members from Frankfurt resigned from the party and joined the provisional committee of the FV. (The Mizrachi central office in Frankfurt was forced to move to Altona as a result.) This new burst of commitment galvanized the FV circle and encouraged them to renew their efforts.[65]

Consequently, a meeting of forty-seven lay leaders from several countries took place in Frankfurt in October, 1911. Its purpose was to create an enlarged provisional committee with a clear mandate and program to achieve an Orthodox world congress. Rosenheim gave the principle address and argued that the task of the organization was no less than

> to bring forth, in an elevated sense, that Jewish unity based on Torah, which yet existed in the middle of the

eighteenth century, before the time of the Enlightenment and the French Revolution. To this extent, the organization as such is a goal in itself.[66]

The organization was thus conceived from the beginning as restorative. The old integral, sacred polity of Judaism with the Torah as its constitution would be renewed amidst the historical upheaval of modernity. Insofar as the organization aims at nothing less than the restoration of Israel's true collective nature, the organization per se constitutes a holy goal. Organization as such has inherent worth.

It also, of course, must have instrumental worth. Thus, programatically speaking, Agudah would have the following practical aims: support of Torah study and Jewish education in general, both in the diaspora and in Palestine; economic support of Jewish communal life in Palestine and in distressed regions of the Diaspora; organization and support of relief work in cases of emergency; as well as supporting literature and a press filled with genuine, Jewish spirit.[67] Rosenheim noted that the Jewish masses would be strengthened by the confidence that a great Jewish organization, which stands on the ground of the Torah, supports them.

Several issues repeatedly arose in the course of the discussion which were to play an enduring role in the life of Agudah. The Western Orthodox were acutely aware of the divisive potential of cultural differences. Not unlike the tension within Zionism between the secular majority and the Orthodox minority, the problem of culture had to be kept in check. The Eastern rabbis were apprehensive lest Western *Bildung* be imported into their yeshivot. Some of the Western leaders were animated by a sense of mission toward the East. Rosenheim essentially followed Herzl's strategy of suspending and postponing cultural debates in order to build basic trust and a shared, practical focus.[68] The sheer differences in modernization within the Orthodox world required a decentralized, federal organization within which the various Jewries would have considerable autonomy.

An equally divisive issue was the extent to which the future organization should become involved in Palestine-oriented projects. As we have already seen, Isaac Halevy's principle aim in conceptualizing the new organization was the support of Orthodoxy in Palestine. Halevy wanted to create an Orthodox competitor of the World Zionist Organization. Rosenheim, it would appear, wanted to do the same, without, however, appearing to emphasize Palestine too much.[69] Rosenheim was undoubtedly impressed by Zionism's claim to represent the Jewish people as such. Symbolically, Agudah, not the Zionist Organization, was to be Israel's true representative before the nations.[70]

The Frankfurt delegates were quite divided over the question of Palestine. Some thought that a rational, modern, systematic approach to the "mitzvah of settling the land of Israel" should be the organization's main contribution. Others were prepared to cooperate with other organizations involved in Palestine work to effectuate this end.[71] Others were convinced that any resemblance to Zionism would destroy the possibility of cooperation with the Eastern rabbinate or detract from Jewish interests in Western Europe.

These potentially divisive concerns were offset by a conviction that the first goal was simply founding the organization as such. The kinds of practical task it would face and the order of priority they would eventually have could be left to the future. In the consensus that emerged, the delegates agreed that close coordination with the East, not only with the rabbis but with the masses, would be necessary. They would not promote the threatening Western synthesis of "torah im derekh eretz." Rabbinic authority would be sought for all important decisions. Indeed, the provisional committee which was formed at the end of the session to plan the next step, an Orthodox world congress, would be expanded to include rabbis.

As the delegates were about to arrive at a final consensus, a brief controversy arose. A motion was offered to amend Rosenheim's preface to the resolution to form Agudah. The original mission statement declared that the delegates agreed to found a "world organization standing *on the ground of the Torah* to solve the common ideal and social tasks of the Jewish totality." Siegmund Fraenkel of Munich proposed that the wording be changed to "on the ground of traditional Judaism" (*auf dem Boden des uberlieferten Judentums*).[72] Rosenheim reacted sharply to this suggestion. He argued, cryptically, that the word "Torah" is not an arbitrarily selected term, but a natural locution ("kein gewähltes sondern ein gewachsenes Wort").[73] Once again, the conservative coloration of Rosenheim's thought, with its preference for organic, evolutionary language gains expression. Suggestions like Fraenkel's, born of the conditions of the present, will not be understood abroad, presumably in the East. Unfortunately, the transcript of the session, terse as it is, affords us little insight into the issues behind this exchange. It is possible that Fraenkel sought to secure a broader foundation for Agudah by invoking the descriptive, generic notion of "traditional Judaism." Rosenheim must have sensed in this a dilution of his rationalized, principled Judaism of the Torah. It is not traditionalism—a sociological category—which unites Orthodoxy. It is the Torah as Grundnorm, as constitution which traditionalism, now raised to conscious self-reflection, affirms as that which unites Orthodoxy. Rosenheim once again stresses the idea as the existence condition of the social reality. If Agudah does not rest on the normativity of the Torah constitution, it will forfeit its claim to be the symbolic representation of the Jewish people per se. The amendment was defeated and the resolution unanimously adopted. Thus, on October 29, 1911, Agudat Israel was, for all intents and purposes, born.

THE KATTOWITZ CONFERENCE AND BEYOND

Between October, 1911 and May, 1912, the Frankfurt-based provisional committee prepared the groundwork for a large gathering of rabbis and lay leaders. The conference was planned for May 27–28, 1912 in Kattowitz (present day Katowice), a German town close to the borders of the Russian and Austro-Hungarian empires where several decades earlier the proto-Zionist Hovevei Zion societies had convened. This juxtaposition of East and West, like much else about the conference, was a piece of carefully designed symbolism.

The Kattowitz conference was intended to present the deliberations of Bad Homburg and Frankfurt to the leaders of East and West, and to formally inaugurate Agudat Israel with suitable publicity and solemnity. Although the invitations to Kattowitz were sent out only in early May, effectively precluding the participation of dignitaries from remote regions such as Rav Kook from Jaffa or Rabbi Bernard Revel from New York, over two hundred persons, more than the desired target, responded positively. The conference could lay claim to definitively representing the Orthodox world.

The invitation itself, synopsizing the prior organizational history of the movement, presented the Bad Homburg and Frankfurt conferences in an interesting, if romanticized light. Frankfurt, it asserted, was a conference of leading Western orthodox laymen, designed to test the viability of the ideas of Israel's luminaries (gaonei Israel) enunciated at Bad Homburg. The reality, as we have seen, was more political and less symmetrical: the rabbis were excluded owing to Breuer's refusal to cooperate with Horowitz and Feist's subsequent pique. This masking of real personal and political antagonisms behind an idealized image of harmonious cooperation was not unusual. The public documents of the movement, while not neglecting the ideological controversies of the members, skirt the personal tensions between them, even when these derive from ideological positions. This, of course, is understandable in propaganda literature. Personalities retreat behind issues, behind the sweep of history and destiny. The participants at Kattowitz fully shared this sense of moment. The movement presented itself as an event of world historical proportions: the true core of the Jewish people, led by the sages of Israel, were rousing themselves from their exilic passivity to organize and act in the name of Torah on the stage of history.

The idea that the sages of Israel orchestrated this renaissance of the Jewish people, was another piece of symbolism. The reality, known to rabbis and laymen alike, that the movement was largely organized and led by activist laymen, was veiled behind the deference and ritualized humility of the laymen. Thus, the provisional committee which drafted the invitation, for example, explicitly states that they have not acted in their own name, but only as agents of the true representatives of Torah and therefore the leaders of *klal Israel*.

The issue of the relationship of rabbis to laymen became an underlying problem in the early phase of the movement. On the one hand, the laymen needed the rabbinate for symbolic reasons. Without a fundamental, constitutionalized status for the rabbinate, the organization would forfeit its claim to being the true representation of the Jewish polity per se. The founding of Agudah did not occur at Frankfurt, despite the wishes of some laymen, as no rabbis were present. On the other hand, the rabbinate clearly got its directions from the laity. Rosenheim at the close of Kattowitz, for example, stressed the need for the rabbinical council to organize itself in order for the work of articulating the movement's statutes and organs to proceed. He offered the names of eleven rabbis for the incipient council and urged them to plan meetings and expand their numbers.[74] In the meantime, the provisional committee would continue its work, stimulating the development of national chapters in various countries. Thus, although the rabbinate received its marching orders from the laity, the laity renounced its own prerogatives in the name of obeying the rabbinate. As in the medieval *kehillah*, potentially conflicting interests were negotiated on the basis of shared agreement about fundamental constitutional principles. The "political" orientation of the laymen deferred to the administrative orientation of the rabbis. Yet such deference could not be complete when crucial constitutional matters were at stake.

Such a constitutional crisis arose at the very moment of Agudah's birth in Kattowitz. Here the fundamentally different orientations toward action threatened to overshadow or imperil consensus. Beginning at Kattowitz and continuing until the first World War, Rosenheim was involved in a daunting conflict with Rabbi Breuer over the so-called "Hungarian demand" that only Jews belonging to separatist congregations could have standing in the movement. This issue ran directly to the heart of the organization's self-definition. Who is a fit Orthodox Jew, that is, who is a loyal citizen of the presumptive Jewish polity? Furthermore, who has the right to decide on the criteria? The problem touched upon the issue of the respective spheres of rabbinic versus lay competence.[75] Rabbi Breuer drew a line in the sand and made this issue a defining, constitutional issue for Agudah and a litmus test of his own authority as a rabbinic decisor. Before considering this issue, an overview of the Kattowitz conference as a whole is necessary.

One gets the impression that Kattowitz was a highly positive experience of encounter between East and West. The Westerners directed hard criticisms against their own communities, lamenting their own secularization, inferiority in Torah learning, and inability to retain the loyalty of their youth. They praised Eastern European Jewry for its piety, intensity, and traditionalism, and repeatedly expressed their need for spiritual nurturance from the East. Any whiff of Western cultural superiority was either carefully repressed or dissipated by a persistent sense of inadequacy in the presence of the Eastern sages. The Easterners, for their part, spoke of their need for the West's organizational skills and charitable powers. They expressed a fear that secular trends were rising in Russia, the Baltic societies and Galicia and that they could learn from the West's experience.[76]

The East's underlying anxiety about the penetration of German secular culture, aside from the Hungarian demand, was the most contentious issue of the conference. Although the Germans in general and Rosenheim in particular always sought to allay their fears with professions of humility and with a firm commitment to abide by the principle of non-interference in local cultural affairs, anxiety remained. The cultural question became acute when a Warsau businessman, Moshe Pfeffer, deeply impressed by what he had learned of Frankfurt's "Torah im derekh eretz" educational system, leapt to the dais and pledged fifty thousand rubles to start a similar school in Warsaw. This burst of impolitic enthusiasm proved deeply embarrassing to the Germans who had tried delicately to wean the Eastern rabbis from their suspicions.[77] Subsequently, Rabbi Chaim Soloveitchik of Brisk summoned Rosenheim and gave him an eighteen point document which made his further participation contingent on Agudah's respecting explicit principles of noninterference in the educational and communal affairs of local *Gemeinden*. This painful experience convinced Rosenheim that beneath the veneer of compatiblity, deep divisions would continue to plague the nascent movement. Both the Lithuanians and the Hungarians were suspicious of the Germans. He feared that should they join forces, the movement would be stillborn.

Rosenheim's fears almost came true as the Hungarian demand played itself out. The Hungarian delegation, in cooperation with Rabbi Salomon Breuer, who was born and trained in Hungary, made their participation contingent on the condition that no one should be allowed to join the Agudah who did not belong to an unimpeachably Orthodox community. In Hungary, this meant that a potential member would have to belong to the national union of state-recognized Orthodox synagogues, which was legally entirely distinct from the non-Orthodox or "neologe" community.[78]

The Hungarian position was born of a bitter experience of intra-Jewish feuding in the nineteenth century. Hungarian Jewry, like German Jewry, had gone through a protracted struggle for emancipation in the course of which a liberal religious, Haskalah-influenced majority professing Magyar nationality displaced traditionalist Orthodoxy. The Reformers or Neologes, as they were called, hoped to implement a consistorial system of compulsory communal membership with their own leadership in control. This policy came close to realization when full Jewish emancipation was achieved in 1867. The Jews were asked by the state to form a congress to create a single, nationwide official Jewish body. The congress convened in 1868, but soon splintered on the issue of whether the Shulchan Arukh would be acknowledged as the basis of Jewish communal life. The Neologe majority, apparently coerced by the Hungarian minister of religion, refused to endorse this position and consequently, the Orthodox minority walked out. The imposition of a countrywide compulsory *Gemeinde* system was averted when the Orthodox sent a delegation to the Austrian kaiser. The resulting settlement left Hungarian Jewry fractured, like German Jewry several years later, into three camps: the Neologe or "Congress Communities," the "Orthodox Communities," and the "Status Quo Communities," which accepted neither innovation.[79] Unlike Germany, however, an Hungarian Jew could not belong to more than one *Gemeinde* at a time. Thus, the division between communities in Hungary was even more complete than it was in Frankfurt, for example. This arrangement, like the German counterpart it partially helped inspire, encouraged a fortress mentality and a principled unwillingness to cooperate among the Orthodox. The Hungarian demand, promoted by Salomon Breuer who had been raised in the Hungarian arrangement and who thought of it as normative, dominated the agenda until the first World War. Indeed, the Hungarian demand was a constitutional crisis of the first order. It hindered the development of the new organization.[80]

The opponents of the Hungarian demand conceived of Agudah as a relatively open, inclusive organization. Some, in keeping with the premise that Agudah was not an Orthodox interest group, but the renascent polity of the Jewish people as such, envisioned an organization open to *all* Jews.[81] Others, perhaps the majority, thought that Agudah should be open to all *Orthodox* Jews who shared its goals. This was Rosenheim's view. He hoped that Agudah could finally provide the umbrella which would allow German Orthodoxy to transcend its parochial, historical divisions and act, in concert with world Orthodoxy, on behalf of *klal Israel*. Rosenheim and others believed that the emergent gestalt of Agudah fundamentally altered the conditions of Orthodox existence and action. The whole did not replace or subsume the parts, but it did transform them. Their opponents did not believe that a new, larger whole altered the basic relation between the preexistent parts. The proponents of Hungarian and Frankfurt separatism could not bear to work on an international level with those whom they considered to be enemies of uncompromising Orthodoxy within their own communities.[82]

The debate at Kattowitz on this question finally came down to the wording of the resolution on founding the Agudah. The original resolution was to read:

> The representatives of Torah-loyal Jewry (*thoratreue Judenheit*) from all of the lands of the diaspora, assembled today in Kattowitz, after hearing the foregoing address declare that "Agudat Israel" is founded and obligate themselves, with all their powers, to work for the building of the organization. The Agudat Israel serves the furtherance of all Jewish interests on a religious basis exclusive of any political tendency.[83]

The Hungarian delegation then made its participation conditional on acceptance of its previous demand that only members of separatist communities, where such exist, could join and proceeded to suggest that the word *thoratreu* be replaced by *strenggläubig-orthodox* (strictly faithful Orthodox). This was immediately opposed by a German delegate, David Hoffmann, rector of the Orthodox seminary in Berlin, on the grounds that "orthodox" makes sense in Hungary or Germany but would have quite a different meaning in Russia, where the term implies Greek Orthodox Christianity. Nonetheless, the Hungarians stood firm. After more debate, Rosenheim proposed that the terms *traditionell-gesetzstreue* (traditional, law-loyal) in German, and *shomrei torah v'mitsvot*, in Hebrew replace the less explicit *torahtreu*. After several delegates who remained in disagreement left the hall, the resolution, as amended was passed.[84]

During the course of the two day's typical parliamentary maneuvers on the floor, R. Breuer had sought to influence the outcome through (no less typical) behind the scenes negotiations. He had convinced the Brisker Rav, R. Soloveitchik, to give his signature to a document certifying that it was an halakhic duty to join a separatist congregation were one available. Soloveitchik had been persuaded by Breuer's argument that if a Catholic community, desirous of attracting Jewish members, had decided to set up kosher institutions such as slaughtering facilities, we would not, nevertheless, consider that community to be a legitimate Jewish community (*tsibbur*). When news spread that Soloveitchik gave his support to Breuer in this way, an hasidic friend of his hurried to him and convinced him that he was not sufficiently apprised of German circumstances to have rendered such a decision. Soloveitchik thereupon withdrew his support, not deigning to involve himself in "deutschen Machlaukes" (German squabbles).[85]

Despite the successful passing of the resolution and thus the formal founding of Agudat Israel, Rosenheim returned to Frankfurt with a heavy heart, well aware that the old divisiveness between separatist and communal Orthodoxy would continue to plague the new organization. In this apprehension, he was completely correct. In practice, the demand of the Hungarian group meant little for Hungarians. Members of Neologe communities or those communities per se would have little interest in joining an organization so massively associated with traditionalist Orthodoxy. With Breuer's sponsorship of the demand, however, the position took on larger consequences for in Frankfurt, unlike Hungary, hundreds of Orthodox Jews, many from Eastern Europe and quite naive about the deutschen Machlaukes, belonged to communal Orthodox congregations. In their small synagogues under the auspices of the main community, they were able to pray with their own landsmen and find a companionship wholly unavailable in the, to them, arch-Germanic, foreign *Religionsgesellschaft*.[86] Rosenheim saw no sense in excluding these potential members on principle. Accordingly, a fierce ideological struggle developed between Rosenheim and his laymen, and the Breuer family.

Salomon Breuer had modified the Hungarian demand to insist that, while membership criteria in Agudah could be relatively flexible, only those members who belonged to separatist communities, where they existed, could run for and be appointed to offices in the organization.[87] Those who had the opportunity to join separatist congregations and did not do so should be thought of "those who have divided themselves from the community" (porshim min ha-tzibbur), a status with invidious halakhic consequences.[88]

Breuer, in his role as halakhic decisor, presented the matter as a purely legal one, thereby trying to deprive the laymen of their standing. But Rosenheim and his associates on the provisional committee demurred. They construed the matter, halakhic complexities notwithstanding, as fundamentally ethical in character thereby claiming a right to contradict their rabbi.[89] Thus a full-blown conflict arose between rabbi and laymen over fundamental constitutional principles. The political orientation stood its ground before an administrative one. Rabbi Breuer took the offensive by sermonizing and writing articles in Orthodox papers. He was also in communication with eastern rabbis and won several over to his cause. The easterners, for their part, were keen to exclude members of Mizrachi from official positions within Agudah. Breuer envisioned an Agudah dominated by a powerful rabbinical council persuaded by his point of view. The rabbinical council, presiding over the anticipated congress of the organization, the Kenesiah Gedolah, would decide on the statutes of the organization. In the event, however, plans to hold a Kenesiah Gedolah were interrupted by the first World War. When the first Kenesiah Gedolah finally took place in 1923, as we shall see, the Hungarian demand failed to influence the statutes.

Rosenheim reacted in the pages of the Israelit, for the first time under his own name, to Salomon Breuer's polemics. He argued that the matter is one of utmost gravity insofar as it has to do not with mere membership in an organization but, mutatis mutandis, with citizenship in the Jewish people.[90] Rosenheim considers the proponents of the demand trapped by a logic that they themselves cannot endorse. They must claim that thousands of eastern European Jews, including Torah scholars, hasidim and others of unimpeachable traditional piety, in the several German cities where Austrittsgemeinden exist are not truly fit to be considered Orthodox Jews. The proponents reached this ad absurdum conclusion because their criterion of what constitutes a community (*tsibbur*) is its elected board, not its constitutive institutions. That is, the fact that the board of the main community is dominated by Reform Jews counts for more on this account than the fact that the community contains many Orthodox synagogues, slaughtering houses, ritual baths, and so on. The composition of the board, rather than other institutional features, defines the constitutional structure of the community.[91]

Rosenheim does not reject the assumption that the board represents and therefore defines the community, terming his opponents' presupposition fundamentally correct (*prinzipiell richtig*). He too takes the concept of representation quite seriously. Whom a community chooses to represent it defines what a community chooses to be. But he argues that there are mitigating circumstances. Throughout the centuries it has been clear, he claims, who can be considered a Jew in good standing and who can not when it comes to things such as Shabbat observance or kashrut. But the matter is vastly more complex when we make standing contingent upon communal membership. For thousands of Orthodox Jews, especially the many immigrants from the East, the details of intra-German rivalries and claims are wholly unknown. Even many German Jews do not know the possibilities and limitiations of communal membership available under the terms of the Prussian *Austrittsgesetz*. And who is to judge either the sincerity of those who do belong to separatist communities or the intentionality of those who do not? Perhaps some belong only in a formal sense and some do not belong due to omission rather than intent. Rosenheim demands that his opponents come down from the realm of legal theory and look to the facts on the ground. The matter is too important to not attend to all of its untidy complexities.[92]

Rosenheim believed that virtually no German Jews had actively chosen not to belong to separatist communities. The vast majority who were members of communal Orthodox congregations were persons of good will who were not sufficiently aware of or persuaded by the separatist ideal and that, furthermore, the fault for this lay with the separatists. The latter had not done enough to make their concept of the *tsibbur* persuasive. Consequently, the intellectual battle for the *tsibbur* must go on, but not at the cost of alienating thousands of honest Jews. Agreeing with the justice of the separatist cause, Rosenheim nonetheless maintained that the philosophical struggle over ideas should not be confused with the moral evaluation of persons. Where persons of genuinely bad character are concerned, the organization should not, at any rate, elect them.

Precisely who could represent Agudat Israel was not formally settled until 1929, when the second Kenesiah Gedolah assembled and the statutes of the organization were finally agreed upon. The first Kenesiah Gedolah was to have taken place in September, 1914, but was interrupted by the outbreak of war.[93] Until the Kenesiah Gedolah, the constitution of Agudah remained deliberately in flux. Thus, the provisional organizational statute of the German *Landesorganisation*:

> Until the acceptance of the final organizational statute of the entire organization, the provisional decisions approved by the assembly at Kattowitz are in force regarding acceptance of membership and the right to be nominated for office.[94]

After the war, Agudah leaders met in Zurich (1919) and in Vienna (the first Kenesiah Gedolah, 1923) in efforts to rebuild the organization and chart a new course in a greatly changed Europe.[95] But the constitutional problem, the minority's pressure to define citizenship in the polity according to separatist criteria, continued to arise. When the statutes for the entire movement were adopted at the second Kenesiah Gedolah the issue of membership was settled in the following way:

> Any Jew, who recognizes the binding nature of the Torah for himself and for the Jewish people can become a member of Agudat Israel. The right belongs to the *Landesorganisation* to set limiting conditions for the acceptance of members for a certain time with the approval of the rabbinical council of the country.[96]

The solution to the problem of eligibility for office was decided in a similar manner:

> Only those members are eligible for election to the organs of Agudat Israel whose convictions and manner of life correspond recognizably to the Torah. Members of organizations which are in principled opposition to Agudat Israel are not eligible for election to the central administrative organs. In controversial cases, the entire rabbinical council will decide concerning a member who belongs to an opposing world organization; the rabbinical council of a country will decide concerning a member who belongs to an opposing organization that relates only to a specific country.[97]

The solution, so typical of Jewish political life, was a consensual compromise based on each side getting less than it hoped for but more than it would have achieved had the other side prevailed. The statutes did not explicitly exclude anyone on the basis of organizational membership. The criteria for belonging were presumably inclusive and rather vague. On the other hand, the rabbinical council at either the highest or at a proximate level could designate certain members unfit for office under certain circumstances. The laymen deferred, (at least in principle) to rabbinic authority, and to the principle of relative regional autonomy or, at least, local custom. Both the federal principle and division of function or power between lay leadership and rabbinate would lead in practice, as we have already seen, to endless controversy and bargaining. A political culture that places primacy on negotiating consensus is typical of covenantal polities. In this, Agudat Israel was no exception to the Jewish rule.

AGUDAT ISRAEL AS THE JEWISH POLITY

We have already seen how Rosenheim thought to legitimate politics by viewing it as an instrument for the realization of Torah. Policy must be grounded on commandments. The only legitimate interest that politics can secure is the interest of Torah. This view both facilitated the pursuit of a rational politics and severely curtailed its scope. But the view implies another paradox as well: the Torah was given to a nation, but it is the responsibility of individuals to fulfil the commandments. Thus there arises in Rosenheim's thought a tension between an organic, corporative conception of the Jewish people, deriving as we have seen from both midrashic and mystical Jewish sources as well as the organic orientation of European conservative thought, and an analytic, contractarian model of nationhood. This tension centrally affects the sense in which Agudah is, symbolically, the Jewish polity.

Isaac Breuer, in his unrelenting critique of Rosenheim, charges that Rosenheim, the quintessential organization man, was actually a pronounced individualist.[98] Rosenheim was, in Breuer's view, fundamentally a modern liberal for whom society was a voluntary and consensual affair, not a primordial, ontological reality. Despite Rosenheim's organic language, his thinking was contractarian. He saw Orthodox Jews outside of the separatist community as "our brothers in Torah and mitzvot." "We have in common with them and their leader 99 percent of Torah and mitzvot and only a single percent separates us."[99] This single percent—the disagreement about community organization—should not stand in the way of cooperative action and organizational unity in an expanded FV.

Isaac Breuer sees this "percent reckoning" as a fundamental betrayal of Hirsch's, that is, the *Jewish*, conception of polity. The Torah cannot be the constitution of the polity unless it is an autonomous organization, untainted by compromise with the liberals and their Orthodox fellow travelers. Rosenheim committed the same error as the Mizrachi: he derogated a fundamental, constitutive matter to a matter of private choice. Thus in Breuer's view, Rosenheim fails to be a social thinker. He fails to rise to an adequate conception of the Jewish people as a primordial collective. He misconceives the nature of their group-being.

Breuer applies this critique to Rosenheim's approach to Palestine. Just as Rosenheim conceived of what separates the

German Orthodox from one another as an essentially individ-
ualistic and numerical matter, so too he saw the commandment of settling the land of Israel as one commandment
among 613: no more (yet no less) important than the others.
For Breuer, by contrast, the Balfour Declaration revealed the
hand of God in history. Something new and revelatory was
happening. Traces of the messiah were appearing amid the
carnage of the Great War.[100] Rosenheim was allegedly unable to
appreciate this profound historical shift because his outlook
was static, ahistorical, numerical.

The issue between Rosenheim and Isaac Breuer was not
entirely philosophical. Rosenheim, as president of the emerging Agudah organization, had to be a statesman who could
keep peace among his various different constituencies. Breuer,
always intellectually radical, was impatient with Rosenheim's
pragmatic, compromising orientation. But Breuer did point to
a real philosophical problem. Rosenheim's basic concept of a
politics of Torah contained, as we have seen, an important
tension.

The warrant for politics, on Rosenheim's view, is the individual's need to fulfil the commandments. The individual cannot fulfil many of the commandments, however, unless the
community helps him or her to do so. Community enters the
picture in a secondary, not a primary or primordial capacity.[101]
Rosenheim thus veers more in the direction of the contractual
pole of Jewish symbolic self-understanding than toward the
organic pole. Yet, as we have repeatedly seen, organic language
and conceptions are not lacking in Rosenheim's understanding
of Jewish peoplehood. While ascriptions of archetypal and
organic nationality occur frequently in Rosenheim's work,
they do not carry over consistently to his characterization of
the Jewish polity. Yet in this too Rosenheim and his Agudah,
perhaps more than Breuer, continue an ancient line of Jewish
political thought. We have seen how both the Bible and the
rabbis, while presenting organic versus contractarian self-def-
initions as ideal-typical constellations of symbols, in practice
tend to fuse and mix them. Whatever is lost in conceptual
purity is compensated for by a more effective, durable frame-

work for self-understanding. Indeed, even the most contractarian of polities, as Rousseau recognized, require an organic, mythic sense of themselves in order to survive.

Thus, the organization that Rosenheim created understood itself to be both a voluntary, consensual, or contractarian society of like-minded individuals and the renewed, organic Jewish sacred polity. Agudah was *klal Israel* fit to act once more on the stage of history. Given such a symbolic self-conception, issues of inclusion and exclusion, as both Isaac Breuer and his father knew, proved crucial: who is an authentic member of the polity, who is not? Who should lead the polity? How should decisions be reached? The early ideological struggles within the organization were over precisely these issues, with Jacob Rosenheim advocating a large, open movement and Salomon Breuer advocating a more exclusive, less compromised one. This basic tension became, as we have seen, a conflict over the proper spheres of lay and rabbinic authority. Such conflicts, divisive as they were, did not pull the movement apart because the parties shared or, under stress, reaffirmed a baseline of consensus about the primacy of the constitution, that is, about the nature of Torah. Their conflict was one of constitutional interpretation and implementation.

Rosenheim reflected on these problems in his address in Zurich in 1919. The Zurich conference represented the first attempt to try to rebuild Agudah after the war.[102] Rosenheim remained committed to organic language: the Jewish *Volk* is an organism with the Torah as its soul. The Council of Torah sages is to be the brain, that is, the seat of the soul. The task is to make the "limbs" of the organism, organs of the Torah.[103] The problem is that this typically conservative image of the polity must be squared with the basically liberal requirements of democracy. Again the tension in Rosenheim's thought. Rosenheim wants to preserve both rule by sages and a free, consensual acceptance of such governance. Similarly, he wants a high level of international unity and enough decentralization so that each country is free to address its own problems in its own nuanced way.[104] Rosenheim's practical suggestion for how to reconcile these conflicting impulses is striking: all groups within Orthodoxy must remain within a democratic dialogue with each other. No group should allow itself to be marginalized. Presumably Rosenheim has in mind groups like Mizrachi or the communal Orthodox. Without being explicit, he implies that if they leave the conversation, hardliners like the Hungarians will come to dominate the organization.[105] Here Rosenheim's high tolerance of pluralism turns into a positive affirmation of pluralistic dialogue, of a culture of negotiation as Agudah's modus vivendi.

Nonetheless, decisions need to be made and conversation eventually must issue into action. At this point, Rosenheim reverts to his fundamental philosophical conviction: politics is nothing more or less than the realization in public life of those ethical and religious ideas addressed in the first instance to individuals. In the Jewish case, these are the ideas of the Torah. Thus, once again, he calls for a high level of consensus on the fundamental task.[106] This openness to unimpeded conversation coupled with deference to religious authority when it comes to decision making recalls the culture of the ancient talmudic academies more than that of a modern parliament although it was clearly influenced by both. Religious conviction will lead to political consensus, he seems to believe.

Rosenheim tried to build consensus through statesmanlike diplomacy, but his main tool was his rhetoric. In his powerful address to the first Kenesiah Gedolah in 1923, he sought the meaning of Agudat Israel against the panorama of the divine creation. God Himself experiences a dialectic of oneness and manifoldness: God is radically unique (kadosh) but His presence (kavod) is also manifest in the manifoldness of creation (malkhuto).[107] Individuals, nations, the historical process all attest to this Presence, but all search for the right way to express, to organize themselves in the light of this presence. The crises of history are struggles between contesting visions of the organization of creation. Israel alone knows how humanity should be organized, as Israel alone received God's constitutional testament, the Torah. Thus, the Jewish people's struggle as individuals and as a nation to overcome the confusion of history—symbolized by the Exile—and the root confusion of the human soul, egoism, forms a mighty religious quest to seek the goals of creation.

Building a unified Agudat Israel partakes of this religious quest. To achieve a unified world organization, is to realize nothing less than what was conceived at Sinai: that the Torah, as the basis of an historical polity, should complete the work of creation. Agudah must strive to commit itself to the love of Israel and the thorough repudiation of the arch-sin of egoism. Thus, Agudah is not a party in any conventional sense. It does not act for its own interests or even less for power. It acts for the values and ideas of its way of life. Ultimately, it acts as the organ of the soul of the Jewish people; of the soul of humanity. It is a messianic vehicle, called to the stage of history in the midst of history's darkest times.[108]

There was a persistent attempt, on the part of the German Agudists, to symbolically represent their organization in this metahistorical, indeed, cosmological fashion. In the midst of building an organization with distinctly political aims, they denied that their movement had anything to do with politics. In the midst of creating a voluntary, consensual movement, they claimed for themselves the most archetypal impulse of necessity: conformity with the will of God. Their organization was but the expression of the eternal people in time, the history of the divine quest for unity realizing itself in history.[109] Thus many Jews who are not pro forma members, the Agudists believed, nonetheless felt themselves to be members of Agudat Israel, that is, they naturally felt that they were members of the Jewish polity to which Agudat Israel gives expression.

To live in history means to be involved in politics. What sort of politics does Agudat Israel profess? A disciple of Rosenheim argued thus: As the embodiment of Torah in public life, as the embodiment and advocate of the true nature of Jewish peoplehood (of the Jewish *Volksbegriff*), Agudat Israel does not want to involve itself in the governmental matters of the host nations. Just as the Jewish people, in its singularity and eternity, is oriented toward a metahistorical sphere that transcends pure historical immanence, so too Agudat Israel is no mere "player" in the political game. It acts in politics as the Jewish people acts in history: to defend itself and its Torah, to safeguard its way of life, to import holiness into the world.[110] Agudat Israel acts in history with one eye fixed beyond history.

Never an end in itself, political action is oriented toward preserving the organic values of the *Volk* and building its utopia in the future. The secular pursuit of order and advantage is transformed into a religious quest for perfection and transcendence. Merely instrumentally rational action is not negated in this view, but subordinated to ethically rational action. This is institutionalized by the subservience of the policy making executive bodies to the Council of Torah Sages. The relative latitude of ends-means calculative action, that is, of rational discretion, vis a vis the supervisory veto power of religious authority would be negotiated again and again in the future history of the organization, just as it had for centuries been negotiated in earlier Jewish polities. In this sense, Agudat Israel was another typical instance of a millenial Jewish political tradition.

CONCLUSION

Agudat Israel conceived of itself, at least initially, in broad political and religious categories. Its membership, committees, and inner structure were to be the Jewish polity in an old/new form. A product of a millenial political tradition and of the specific social and cultural milieux of East and West in the late nineteenth century, it fused, as do all products of Jewish creativity, distinctive Jewish contents with the features of the contemporary, general environment.

These latter include, first and foremost, a widespread modern longing for community, for *Gemeinschaft*, to use Tonnies's famous opposition, in the midst of *Gesellschaft*. What distinguishes the religiously informed longing for *Gemeinschaft* is the requirement that the community relate to a sacred center of power and orientation; that community mediate the forces of the sacred center to the mundane, disenchanted periphery. In the biblical traditions of activist, rational religiosity, the relationship to the center is realized in action rather than in contemplation. Model communities must be created in which men and women can orient their public and private lives to eternally valid, transcendent norms.

The Agudists perceived Jewish history as having fallen off its divinely ordained track. They wanted their activist community to set it straight again, first by properly organizing themselves, then by modeling their synthesis to the world at large. They claimed for their model the status of the Jewish polity as such: the ideal or normative template for the organization of *klal Israel* in history. Rosenheim, in fidelity to this idea, sought to keep Agudah as open to potential "citizens" as possible. If Agudah is to be the symbolic political representation of the Jewish people, then it must, in principle, be open to all Jews who acknowledge the Torah as the national constitution. This orientation was both old and new: old, insofar as it derived from midrashic and kabbalistic organic ways of understanding the nature of the Jewish people; new, insofar as European conservatism's use of organic language for national self-description provided an intellectual context for the selection and application of the Jewish concepts. Rosenheim's orientation, as we have seen, was both old and new in other ways. In part, his understanding of the Jewish people as a voluntaristic, contingent group reflects the ancient covenantal understanding of Israelite origins. In part, his orientation reflects the liberal-bourgeois commitment to *Bildung*: Agudah posited a social-cultural ideal which it would spread noncoercively through example, through education. Agudah would model an ideal, voluntaristic community of thinkers who subscribed to the same principles. Citizenship in its polity was a matter of choice and deliberation, not fate. It would persuade and educate the Jews to embrace their ancient constitution and live in fidelty to it on a national level.

This noncoercive, *Bildung*-oriented focus was, perhaps, a luxury reserved for a group which was not political in the narrowest sense, that is, a group which could not aspire to sharing power in a sovereign state. In actual fact, Agudah, at least in Germany, remained a *Verein*, an interest group, lobby and self-help society. The limitedness of its political influence is in inverse proportion to the enormity of its symbolic claims. Even as an actual Jewish political party in Poland, it could do little more than act as a lobby, albeit within parliament, for Orthodox interests. Rosenheim's liberal ideal of a noncoercive, educational approach was well-suited to the very limited range of political opportunity available to Agudah. It was not, unfortunately, well suited to the ineducable, increasingly anti-Semitic European societies in which Agudah had to function.

There are many modern groups, often called "fundamentalist," which arose from impulses not unlike those that gave rise to Agudah, which do have access to positions of control in sovereign states. Such groups rely less on education and the modelling of a transcendent communal ideal than they do on the conquest of political territory, either through revolution, as in Iran, or through democratic processes, as in the United States. Yet curiously, when Agudah had the opportunity to participate in positions of power within a sovereign state, Israel, it continued to act more as a lobby for ultra-Orthodox interests than as the presumed representation of *klal Israel* as such. It abandoned its self-representation as the Jewish polity per se and settled for the minor role cast for it by its opponents. Isaac Breuer, who hoped for an halakhic theocracy in the land of Israel, was perhaps the last holdout for the maximalist Agudah ideal and even he moderated his hopes at the end of his life in 1946.

Thus it seems that the liberal-bourgeois ideal of secular democracy, a product of the modern Enlightenment, at least in this one case, overwhelmed a version of polity which self-consciously blended secular modern and ancient sacred elements. Although Agudah sought to overcome the disenchantment of modern social life and its narrowed political vision it eventually accomodated itself to that disenchantment and adapted itself to the shrunken political vision of modernity. Its version of ancient sacred community lives on in a compartmentalized fashion vis-a-vis the secular modern world. The Orthodox Jews whom Agudah represents today do not expect their politics to be sacral in any sense. The sacred is reserved for the charmed circle of family and synagogue. Elsewhere disenchantment is allowed to reign. Politics is reserved for the most utilitarian and unavoidable concerns.

Why did the Agudist vision of a sacred politics, a politics as religious experience die? A full consideration of this problem would require further historical study of Agudah's post-World War II career in Israel and in the United States, without which only the most tentative speculations can be made. Nonetheless, in line with the main assumptions and findings of this study, I would offer the following suggestion. The German ideologues of Agudah had significantly underestimated, I argued, the rational, disenchanting dimensions always implicit in the Jewish political tradition. Their religious vision of a redemptive politics shaped by rabbinic sages from halakhic sources was rooted in the tradition, but was also a misreading of the tradition. The typically modern yearning for a rational utopia, so prevalent in the political ideologies of the late nineteenth century, overwhelmed the delicate balance the Jewish political tradition had struck between the different types of action. In the end, the reality of politics, which the Jewish political tradition long recognized, caught up with the utopian, almost messianic enthusiasm of Agudah's Western founders.

This is not to say that their hope that Agudah would be acknowledged as the reborn Jewish polity was mere fantasy. The choice is not between a completely disenchanted politics of probity and a politics of fantasy. On the contrary, many modern states have their cake and eat it too. Rationalized and liberal societies such as Great Britain continue to have hereditary monarchies in which repose the symbolic essence of the nation. Such political symbols have a religious reach. They point to where the sacred touches the nation, simultaneously insuring its connection with an eternal, higher power and depriving the normal mechanisms of government from that connection. In this way, political society both participates in transcendence and is marked off from it.

Modernity no less than the millenial Jewish experience is therefore, in principle, open to a politics that is capable of both the requisite level of rationality and pragmatism and a transcendence seeking dynamic. There is no reason to think that this openness will abate. If anything, modern men and women in the liberal societies seem ever more hungry for some new articulation of this balance. Thus, it is not inconceivable that something like the Agudist version of the Jewish polity might one day reemerge in a national Jewish dialogue on the nature of religion and public order. Although public debate on religious questions in Israel has often been poisoned by the legacy of partisan politics, the secular sphere has shown some openness toward the need for a post-Zionist, post-liberal philosophical orientation. It does not seem likely today that Agudat Israel could rediscover or reaffirm the ideals of its youth and contribute to such a national conversation. But to the extent that the Jews as a nation continue to turn to Torah as the mirror in which they see themselves, something like the impulse which gave rise to Agudah will always stir within them.

INTRODUCTION

1. Wilfred Cantwell Smith, *The Meaning and End of Religion* (Minneapolis: Fortress Press, 1991), esp. chap. 2.

2. Spinoza is treated infra, p. 35. On Kant's view, cf. *Religion Within the Limits of Reason Alone*, Theodore M. Green and Hoyt H. Hudson, trans. (New York: Harper Torchbooks, 1960) p. 116ff.

3. Allan Arkush, *Moses Mendelssohn and the Enlightenment* (Albany: State University of New York Press, 1994), p. 228.

4. The extreme of methodological cynicism (religion as nothing-but-ideology) is a more prevalent problem than fideism, but both are to be avoided. The first is reductionistic, while the second cuts off inquiry. The methodology that gives the widest latitude to the irreducibility of religious self-understanding is phenomenology of religion. Its internal problem is how to cope with fideism. Some phenomenologists, so-called essentialists, believe that religious discourse, symbols, practices, and so on, refer to a real, transcendental dimension which is, in itself, unknowable. Others, so-called historical-typological phenomenologists, bracket out the metaphysical issue of reference and write in an als-ob mode, that is, they identify with the discourse of their subjects as if it were true. This latter stance is the one taken here. Cf. Sumner B. Twiss and Walter H. Conser, Jr. *Experience of the Sacred* (Hanover, NH: Brown University Press, 1992), Introduction; cf. also Hans H. Penner, "Is Phenomenology a Method for the Study of Religion?" *Bucknell*

Review, vol. 18, Winter 1970, no. 3, pp. 29–54. Penner criticizes the incoherence of the essentialist version of phenomenology of religion. Agreeing with his criticism, I would underscore that phenomenology of religion is no more and no less than a conceptual tool. It is not itself a mode of religious experience. In this sense, it is compatible with another methodological tool, the ideal type. Cf. infra. p. 73.

5. "Band" or "union" should be supplemented by the observation that the parties to the union continue to retain their own integrity, implying that an agudah is a federation. As to the transliteration of the Hebrew term, I follow the standard modern Israeli pronounciation. The German Jews used "Agudas Jisroel." The Yiddish designation is "Agudos Yisroel." By refering to the German Jews as "orthodox" and the Eastern European Jews as "traditionalists," I mean to call attention to the sociological fact that Orthodoxy is a rational system of religious thought and practice worked out in dialectical response to religious liberalism. This reflects the history of Judaism in the post-Enlightenment period. The East, by contrast, retained a less self-conscious, more immediate traditionalism. Cf. Karl Mannheim," Conservative Thought," in Kurt Wolff, ed., *From Karl Mannheim* (New York: Oxford University Press, 1971), p. 173.

6. Ezra Mendelsohn, *On Modern Jewish Politics* (New York: Oxford University Press, 1993), pp. 52, 59.

7. Donald Smith, *Religion and Political Development* (Boston: Little, Brown & Co., 1970), p. xi.

8. Alfred Döblin, *Journey to Poland*, Joachim Neugroschel, trans. (New York: Paragon House, 1991), p. 59.

9. That the easterners wanted a limited, practical politics and the westerners instigated a more revolutionary framework of self-definition (at least in a symbolic sense) upsets the conventional historical paradigm in terms of which western Jewish politics was assimilationist and therefore minimalistic while eastern Jewish politics was revolutionary and transformative. Cf. Jonathan Frankel, "Modern Jewish Politics East and West (1840–1939): Utopia, Myth, Reality," in Zvi Gitelman, ed. *The Quest for Utopia: Jewish Political Ideas and Institutions Through the Ages* (Armonk, New York: M. E. Sharpe, Inc., 1992), pp. 81–84. For a concise overview of Agudah as a party in the State of Israel see Gary Schiff, *Tradition and Politics*:

The Religious Parties of Israel (Detroit: Wayne State University Press, 1977). Schiff traces the decline of the theocratic ideal and its adjustments to the realities of actual political participation in a Jewish state.

10. Jacob Katz, "Orthodoxy in Historical Perspective." in Peter Y. Medding, ed., *Studies in Contemporary Jewry*, vol. 2 (Bloomington: Indiana University Press, 1986) p. 9.

11. Gershon C. Bacon "The Politics of Tradition: Agudat Israel in Polish Politics, 1916–1939" in Peter Y. Medding, ed. *Studies in Contemporary Jewry*, vol 2., p. 145.

12. See note 11 above, p. 151

13. See note 11 above, p. 152; cf. note 6 above, pp. 71–72.

14. For a nuanced typology of Orthodox community structures, cf. Joseph Carlebach, *Das Gesetztreue Judentum* (Berlin: Schocken Verlag, 1936), pp. 51–54.

15. Cf., for example, Isaac Breuer, *Sha'ali Serufah: Zur Erinnerung an das deutsche Judentum* (Jerusalem: Mossad Yitzhak Breuer, 1979), p. 163

16. Joseph Carlebach, *Das Gesetztreue Judentum*, p. 43. To say that Orthodoxy had a distinctly political conception of Judaism requires a nuance. Samson Raphael Hirsch, for the purpose of arguing the cause of an independent Orthodoxy before the German state authorities, presented Orthodoxy as a confession. That is, he had to *deny* that the official Jewish community, the Gemeinde, had an obligatory, binding political character. By presenting Judaism as a faith, he could argue that Reform Judaism and Orthodox Judaism had so little in common that they were two separate faiths. Consequently, they should not be forced to live together in one community enforced by state coercion. Such a community contradicts the right to an enlightened freedom of religion. Thus Hirsch appears to relegate community per se, that is, a political conception of Judaism, to the medieval past. Mordechai Breuer has argued that this was merely a political strategy on Hirsch's part. Indeed Hirsch's theory of community, as we shall see in chapter 2, undermines his confessionalistic rhetoric. Mordechai Breuer, *Jüdische Orthodoxie im Deutschen Reich 1871–1918* (Frankfurt/Main: Jüdischer Verlag bei Athenäum, 1986), p. 266.

17. The term "theocracy" must be used with caution. Shimon Federbush rejects the term because, in modern usage, it implies rule by clerics. (Cf. his *Mishpat ha-Melukha b'Yisrael* (Jerusalem: Mossad Harav Kook, 1973) p. 26ff). Properly understood however, the term—as intended by its coiner, Josephus—indicates the Jews'preference for direct rule by God, rather than by earthly rulers. Direct rule by God, mediated by the Torah, is what theocracy denotes in our context. Cf. Jacob Rosenheim, "Konstituierung des Zentralrates," *Blätter* (Frankfurt am Main: Gruppenverband der Palästina-Zentrale und der Jugend-Organisation der Agudas Jisroel für Deutschland, 1921), p. 1. Rosenheim states that the rabbis do not want to rule, but simply to make legal decisions "according to the divine law in the name of the King who rules in Jeshurun." For Josephus cf. *Contra Apionem*, bk. 2, 17.

18. This discussion follows that of David Sorkin in *The Transformation of German Jewry 1780–1840*, (New York: Oxford, 1987), chap. 1.

19. George Mosse, *German Jews Beyond Judaism*, (Bloomington: Indiana University Press and Cincinnati: Hebrew Union College Press, 1985), p. 4.

20. See note 19 above, p. 16.

21. Quoted in Jehuda Reinharz, *Fatherland or Promised Land: The Dilemma of the German-Jew, 1893–1914*, (Ann Arbor: University of Michigan Press, 1975), p. 72.

22. See note 21 above, pp. 73–74.

23. See note 21 above, p. 75.

24. Cf. the discussion in Mordechai Breuer, *Jüdische Orthodoxie im Deutschen Reich*, 1871–1918, (Frankfurt/M: Jüdischer Verlag bei Athenäum, 1986), pp. 272–279.

25. The sermon is translated and reprinted in Samson Raphael Hirsch, *Judaism Eternal*, I. Grunfeld, ed. and trans., (London: Soncino Press, 1956), p. 126.

26. See note 25 above, p. 129.

27. After summarizing various duties to the State, he adds: "But this outward obedience to the laws must be joined by an inner obedience: i.e. to be loyal to the State with heart and mind, loyal to

the kings, to guard the honour of the State with love and pride, to strive with enthusiasm wherever and whenever you can so that the nation's institutions shall prosper, so that every aim which your country has set as its national goal shall be achieved and furthered . . . And this duty is an unconditional duty and not dependent upon whether the State is kindly intentioned towards you or harsh. Even should they deny your right to be a human being and to develop a lawful human life upon the soil which bore you—*you* shall not neglect your duty." Samson Raphael Hirsch, *Horeb: A Philosophy of Jewish Laws and Observances*, I. Grunfeld, ed. and trans., (London: Soncino, 1962), p. 462.

28. Mordechai Breuer, *Jüdische Orthodoxie im Deutschen Reich*, p. 34.

29. H. H. Gerth and C. W. Mills, *From Max Weber* (New York: Oxford University Press, 1978), p. 51.

30. Jacob Rosenheim, *Agudistische Schriften* (Frankfurt/Main: Verlag des Israelit und Hermon, 1929) p. 114. On organic metaphors in Judaism cf. Jacob Katz, *Tradition and Crisis*, Bernard Dov Cooperman, trans. (New York: New York University Press, 1993), p. 170.

31. Clifford Geertz, *Local Knowledge* (New York: Basic Books, 1983), p. 124.

32. See n. 30, p. 164.

33. Eric Hobsbawm and Terence Ranger, eds., *The Invention of Tradition* (Cambridge: Cambridge University Press, 1989), cf. esp. p. 263ff.

34. S. N. Eisenstadt, "Post-Traditional Societies and the Continuity and Reconstruction of Tradition," *Daedalus*, Winter 1973, pp. 1–27. Cf. also Samuel P. Huntington, "The Change to Change: Modernization, Development, and Politics," *Comparative Politics* 3, April 1971, pp. 283–322.

35. The central work for our purposes is Edward Shils's, *Tradition* (Chicago: University of Chicago Press, 1981).

CHAPTER 1

1. *Agudas Jisroel: Berichte und Materialien* (Frankfurt am Main: Provisorischen Comité der "Agudas Jisroel," 1912?), p. 63.

2. On Weber's conception of ideal types cf. Max Weber, *The Methodology of the Social Sciences*, Edward A. Shils and Henry A. Finch, trans. (Glencoe,IL: The Free Press, 1949).

3. Baron's problem had much to do with his definition of politics, dependent as it was on the nation state. He writes: "This [rabbinic Judaism's "democracy of learning"] is but one example of the inapplicability of general political categories to Jewish communal history. Long before the full evolution of its diaspora community the Jewish people had become a basically non-political entity. Indeed, in its long diaspora career it had demonstrated the independence of the essential ethnic and religious factors from the political principle. Through a concatenation of unique historical circumstances, it early learned to discard *the general acceptance of state supremacy* and to proclaim in theory, as well as to live in reality, the supremacy of religious, ethical and ethnic values. That is why a purely political interpretation, even of the constitutional life of the Jewish community, will do less than justice to the nonpolitical core of the problem." pp. 28–29, (italics my own)
Baron's position is actually more nuanced than a simple reduction of political life to state sovereignty. He is making a polemical point against the associated ideological protagonists of a Soviet-style *Volksgemeinde*, such as the secular, political community instituted by the Soviets in Birobidjian. Without Hebrew, Zionism, and religious life such a community was doomed, as Baron correctly foresaw, to fail. (cf. p. 16) Salo Baron, *The Jewish Community*, vol. 1 (Philadelphia: Jewish Publication Society of America, 1948). For a Christian parallel to this way of cutting the distinction between state and society or community cf. Ernst Troeltsch, *The Social Teachings of the Christian Churches*, Olive Wyon, trans. (New York: Macmillan, 1931), pp. 31–34.

4. For Strauss's distinction, cf. Leo Strauss, *What is Political Philosophy?* (Chicago: University of Chicago Press, 1988), pp. 12–13. For examples of rabbinic "political thought" consult Martin Sicker, *The Judaic State: A Study in Rabbinic Political Theory* (New York: Praeger, 1988). Sicker, drawing on halakhic and traditional exegetical literature, attempts to present a rabbinic "theory" of politics. An imaginative compilation of primary sources, the text systematizes traditions into a more coherent, theoretically grounded whole than rabbinic thought allows. Cf. Martin Yaffe's critical review of Sicker in *Canadian Philosophical Review*, 9 (1989), pp. 72–75. Gordon

Freeman similarly tries to present a coherent account of the rabbinic understanding of the political, albeit with more of a sense of the methodological problems involved. Gordon Freeman, *The Heavenly Kingdom: Aspects of Political Thought in the Talmud and Midrash* (Lanham, MD: University Press of America, 1986). Both of these texts may be understood as presentations of traditions of practical reasoning on political matters. Jacob Neusner's *Rabbinic Political Theory* (Chicago: University of Chicago Press, 1991) reconstructs the political thought of the Mishnah using Weberian categories. Other systematizing works on Jewish political tradition include Daniel J. Elazar, editor's *Authority, Power and Leadership in the Jewish Polity* (Lanham, MD: University Press of America, 1991), *Morality & Power: Contemporary Jewish Views* (Lanham, MD: University Press of America, 1990), and *Kinship and Consent: The Political Tradition and Its Contemporary Uses* (Lanham, MD: University Press of America, 1983). For basic texts from Maimonides and Abravanel with brief commentaries, cf. Ralph Lerner and Muhsin Mahdi, eds., *Medieval Political Philosophy* (New York: The Free Press, 1963), pp. 188–270.

5. On Abravanel's dependence on contemporary Christian writers, note especially Leo Strauss, "On Abravanel's Philosophical Tendency and Political Teaching," J. B. Trend and H. Loewe, eds., *Isaak Abravanel* (Cambridge: Cambridge University Press, 1937). A less polemical study of Abravanel's sources is Herbert Finkelscherer, "Die Quellen und Motive der Staats—und Gesellschaftsauffassung des Don Isaak Abravanel," MGWJ, vol. 81, 1937, pp. 496–508. Maimonides' political philosophy is discussed in Gerald Blidstein, *Political Concepts in Maimonidean Halakha* (Hebrew), (Israel: Bar Ilan University Press, 1983), pp. 93–96. Cf. also Ralph Lerner, "Moses Maimonides," in Leo Strauss, ed., *The History of Political Philosophy* (Chicago: University of Chicago Press, 1972), pp. 203–23 and Leo Strauss, *What is Political Philosophy?* (Glencoe, IL: The Free Press, 1959), pp. 155–69.

6. Israel Schepansky, *The Takkanot of Israel*, vol. 4 (Hebrew) (Jerusalem: Mossad Ha-Rav Kook, 1993), p. 219. Schepansky typifies what we shall later call the "administrative" orientation. Politics is severely restrained, from this point of view, by the halakha. The political agent is given a tightly limited domain for action by the halakhic authorities. His sphere of activity is foreordained by the Torah.

7. Eli Lederhendler, "Modern Jewish Politics," in Jack Wertheimer, ed., *The Modern Jewish Experience: A Reader's Guide* (New York: New York University Press, 1993), p. 181.

8. Daniel J. Elazar, *Community & Polity: the Organizational Dynamics of American Jewry* (Philadelphia: Jewish Publication Society of America, 1976), pp. 5–6. Cf. also Jonathan Frankel, "Modern Jewish Politics East and West," pp. 81–82.

9. Lederhendler, "Modern Jewish Politics," p. 182.

10. Elazar, *Community and Polity*, p. 5; cf. Allan Arkush, *Moses Mendelssohn and the Enlightenment*, chaps. 6–7.

11. David Biale notes that Elazar "uses a particular vocabulary, drawn from classical sources. In his introduction, Elazar defines this vocabulary: Jewish political life is always organized around the concept of covenant (brit); the Jewish polity is always a permutation of the biblical edah; and political power is always divided in a 'federal' system defined by the three crowns mentioned in the mishnaic tractate Avot . . . Those who use this vocabulary and the model it describes tend to approach this Jewish political phenomena as political scientists: they attempt to fit the historical data into the a priori model." While Biale affirms the heuristic role of attempting to elucidate a "continuous Jewish political theory based on the Bible," he is concerned that "the effort to find continuities often seems to me to evade the equally important discontinuities that characterize Jewish history." This inattention to discontinuity, the result of an alleged noninductive, aprioristic method is the core of Biale's critique of Elazar. Cf. David Biale, review of *Authority, Power and Leadership in the Jewish Polity: Cases and Issues*, Daniel J. Elazar, ed., (Lanham, MD: Jerusalem Center for Public Affairs and University Press of America, 1991) in *Jewish Political Studies Review*, vol. 5:1–2, Spring 1993, pp. 134–37.

12. Leo Strauss,"Maimonides' Statement on Political Science," in *What is Political Philosophy?*, p. 157. For an early statement of Strauss's on how Maimonides contextualized his political thought within his religious thought cf. "Der Ort der Vorsehungslehre nach der Ansicht Maimunis," *Monatsschrift für Geschichte und Wissenschaft des Judentums*, vol. 81, 1937, p. 96. Cf. also Kenneth Hart Green, *Jew and Philosopher: The Return to Maimonides in the Jewish Thought of Leo Strauss* (Albany: State University of New York Press, 1993), esp. chap. 5.

13. One might say that Rosenzweig ignored Judaism's own political voices. He assumed with Hegel and German Historicism that the State is the bearer of politics and that history is the history of states. Lacking a state, the Jews are neither political nor historical.

14. Leo Strauss, *Philosophy and Law*, Fred Baumann, trans. (Philadelphia: Jewish Publication Society, 1987), p. 25.

15. Yitzhak Baer, in an effort to establish the national and political—rather than narrowly religious—character of Jewish existence locates the traditions of the Mishna in the Hasmonean period. He views the Mishna as a social and political document: the constitution of the Jewish version of the polis. Cf. H. H. Ben-Sasson and S. Ettinger, eds., *Jewish Society Throughout the Ages* (New York: Schocken Books, 1973), p. 72, and "The Origins of Jewish Communal Organization in the Middle Ages," Zipporah Brody, trans., in *Binah: Studies in Jewish History*, vol. 1, Joseph Dan, ed. (New York: Praeger, 1989).

16. Louis Finkelstein, *Jewish Self-Government in the Middle Ages*, reprint edition (Westport: Greenwood Press, 1975).

17. *Theologico-Political Treatise*, in R. H. M. Elwes, trans. *Chief Works of Benedict de Spinoza* (New York: Dover, 1951), chap. 5, pp. 75–76.

18. See note 17 above, chap. 17, p. 232ff., chap. 18, p. 240.

19. See note 17 above, chap. 3, p. 56.

20. Gershon Weiler, *Jewish Theocracy* (Leiden: E.J. Brill, 1988), p. 10.

21. See note 20 above, p. 99. For Spinoza's (positive?) appreciation of some aspects of biblical polity, cf. *Theologico-Political Treatise*, chap. 17, p. 240.

22. Weiler's reading of history is tied to a contemporary critique of religion in the political culture of Israel. Following Spinoza, Weiler sees a radical incompatibility between a rational, prudential and liberal politics and the culturally salient presence of Judaism. In his view, the Jewish tradition of "anti-politics" is an absolute threat to the State of Israel. Weiler's view is one of extreme and consistent secularism, one might say in a precise way, of anti-Judaism. Ibid., see especially chaps. 1–5.

23. D. Elazar and S. Cohen, *The Jewish Polity* (Bloomington: Indiana University Press, 1984); D. Elazar, "Covenant as the Basis of the Jewish Political Tradition," *The Jewish Journal of Sociology*, vol. 10, no. 1 (June 1978); S. Cohen, "The Concept of The Three *Ketarim*: Its Place in Jewish Political Thought and Its Implications for a Study of Jewish Constitutional History," *AJS Review*, vol. 9, no. 1 (Spring 1984).

24. Elazar, "Covenant as the Basis," p. 5.

25. David Biale, *Power and Powerlessness in Jewish History* (New York: Schocken Books, 1987), pp. 5–8. Cf. also Ismar Schorsch, "On the History of the Political Judgment of the Jew," Leo Baeck Memorial Lecture, no. 20 (New York: Leo Baeck Institute, 1976).

26. See note 25 above, p. 215.

27. See note 25 above, ch. 2.

28. See note 25 above, p. 206.

29. See note 25 above, p. 17.

30. David Biale, *Gershom Scholem: Kabbalah and Counterhistory*, (Cambridge: Harvard University Press, 1979) p. 211.

31. See note 30 above, p. 201.

32. See note 30 above, p. 2.

33. Biale believes that this position is nonrelativistic because although Judaism, conceived as an anormative conjunction of opposites, is in principle open to infinite permutations, in reality it is finite. That is to say, certain possibilities have been rejected in the historical process. But this does not rescue anarchism from relativism because it ascribes no normative weight to those possibilities which became historical actualities. They are treated as facts, not values. On the other hand, Scholem does have a normative agenda, as Biale, and more recently, Moshe Idel point out. He stood for a humanistic Zionism, butressed by a vitalist philosophy. His embrace of vitalism led him to disparage the legal/rational framework of Judaism and to privilege the forces of will and being, thus producing a representation of what must be reclaimed for Judaism to survive. This blurring of the fact/value distinction is, as Biale admits, "fraught with difficulties." Yet Biale minimizes these difficulties

by asserting that, after all, Scholem was an historian, not a philosopher and his work need not be judged by its philosophical consistency. This seems entirely too weak a justification of Scholem's
standpoint and hermeneutics. The strongest defense is probably Karl
Mannheim's claim that the worry about relativism is an issue only
for those with the expectation that there exists a fixed position in the
first place. Unless such ultimate truth can be ascertained things are
not right. Mannheim attributes this belief to a bad epistemology in
which all propositions about the human situation need to have the
fixity of 2+2=4. Relativism is dissolved by the insight that all knowledge is inherently relational and that truth can be approximate, not
ultimate, and still be truth. On this view, Scholem's value laden
historiography can still be productive of truth, indeed, its produc-
tivity is heightened by the value-driven questions he asked of the
historical material. (Biale, ibid., pp. 201–05; Karl Mannheim,
*Ideology and Utopia: An Introduction to the Sociology of
Knowledge*, Edward Shils and Louis Wirth, trans. (New York:
Harcourt, Brace, 1936). Mannheim (and Scholem!) are open to precisely the same critique as Leo Strauss gave Max Weber. Cf. Leo
Strauss, *Natural Right and History*, chap. 2.

34. This discussion follows the observations of Edward Shils in
his *Tradition* (Chicago: University of Chicago Press, 1981) p. 168.

35. The issue of the extent of a legitimately secular sphere in
Judaism, that is, of a domain of rational politics, will be explored in the
next chapter. Preliminarily, we can claim that there is a bounded, that
is, discretionary domain wherein political choices and experimentation are valid. This discretionary sphere (discretion, according to Ronald
Dworkin, is like a hole in a doughnut) is circumscribed by the normative universe of the Torah. Even when actors within the "hole" make
rationally-based choices, they must justify them by reference to the
authoritative norms of the "doughnut." Cf. Ronald Dworkin, "The
Model of Rules," in Joel Feinberg and Hyman Gross, eds., *Philosophy of
Law* (Belmont: Wadsworth Publishing Co., 1975), p. 84.

36. Alisdaire MacIntyre, "Traditions and Conflicts," *Liberal
Education*, vol. 73:5, November/December 1987.

37. David Biale, *Power and Powerlessness*, p. 29

38. TB Sanhedrin 5a. In context, this text is arguing the superior
authority of the Exilarchate of Babylonia against the claims of the

Patriarchate in the land of Israel. There is a fundamental problem of constitutional authority which the rabbis are using exegesis, that is, constitutional interpretation, to adjudicate.

39. *Bet ha-Behirah*, Sanhedrin 52b. Quoted from Menachem Elon, *Jewish Law: History, Sources, Principles*, Bernard Auerbach and Melvin Sykes, trans., vol. 1 (Philadelphia: Jewish Publication Society, 1994), p. 59.

40. Cited in Israel Schepansky, *The Takkanot of Israel* (Hebrew), vol. 4 (Jerusalem: Mossad Ha-Rav Kook, 1993), p. 3. Cf. similar utterances by Nachmanides and Simeon ben Zemach Duran ad loc.

CHAPTER 2

1. For our purposes, the term "polity" is more exact than the more common "community" insofar as polity designates a stronger, more obligatory form of social life than community does. Polity connotes a social structure with political dimensions such as law making and an authority that can coerce or at least obligate. Community, in contemporary usage, suggests a more voluntary and transitory form of association. (Indeed, community is now used euphemistically to designate any form of association, even imaginary ones such as the "virtual community" of computer network enthusiasts.) On the other hand, polity ought not to be confused with "state," a term which, in modernity, has monopolized the political sphere for itself. Indeed, the modern state with its centralization of power and authority is based on the effective elimination and cooptation of lesser centers of power.

Polity derives from the Greek word *politeuma* which designated the self-governing ethnic communities of the Hellenistic world, including those of the Jews. I shall use polity here when I want to designate a strong form of community with a high level of political obligation, an explicit constitutional basis and an imagined inner connection to ancient Jewish norms and institutions.

2. For a typology of legitimating frameworks see Douglas Sturm, "Corporations, Constitutions and Covenants: On Forms of Human Relation and the Problem of Legitimacy," *Journal of the American Academy of Religion*, vol. 41, 1973. pp. 345–46.

3. One might object that these questions derive from a false dichotomy; that both rational calculations and religious values/legitimation are fully compatible with one another; indeed, that halakha is an instrument peculiarly well-fitted to reconciling ideal and practical courses of action within the prevailing social realities. This is basically true. Jewish law allows for spheres of discretion in which duly constituted authorities such as halakhic decisors, on the one hand, and civil officers such as the king, elders and community leaders, on the other hand, are empowered to legislate. Such legislation (*takkanot* or *gezerot*) expands and contracts, and sometimes contradicts established Torah law, yet nevertheless remains valid. The expansion of the discretionary sphere and thus the rise in importance of *takkanot* in communal goverance from the tenth century onwards occasioned much analysis and theorizing among halakhic scholars on the implicit theory that legitimizes this "secular" sphere. Cf. Menachem Elon, *Jewish Law*, vol. 2, Bernard Auerbach and Melvin Sykes, trans., (Philadelphia: Jewish Publication Society, 1994), chaps. 13, 14, 18, 19. Also: Gerald Blidstein, "'Ideal' and 'Real' in the Classical Jewish Polity," Zvi Gitelman, ed., *The Quest for Utopia:Jewish Political Ideas and Institutions Through the Ages* (Armonk, NY: M. E. Sharpe, Inc., 1992).

Yet the point is not simply that halakha makes room for a polity to function in the real world, but that as the polity functions fundamentally different orientations persist among its leaders. I would still argue, at the level of ideal types, that we are dealing with two tendencies. The one ideal is of an empowered rationality that is not indifferent to coherence with the halakhic system, but nevertheless does seek its own level. The other ideal is that of a traditional authority that insists on the necessity of making rational decisions cohere with inherited norms. The reality of decision making in the polity is a sometimes harmonious blend and at other times a confrontation between these two impulses.

4. For the theoretical basis of the distinction between politics and administration see Karl Mannheim, *Ideology and Utopia*, Louis Wirth and Edward Shils, trans., (New York: Harcourt, Brace and World, 1936) pp. 112–117. Cf. also Max Weber, "Politics as a Vocation," in Hans Gerth and C. Wright Mills, eds., *From Max Weber* (New York: Oxford University Press, 1946). This distinction is somewhat problematic, but still, I think, helpful. It is problematic insofar as it grows out of the European context of a centralized, rei-

fied State where decision making (politics) is monopolized by a powerful center and a bureaucratic periphery (administration) merely
implements the center's decisions. That model is clearly inappro-
priate to our context. Nonetheless, insofar as the distinction cap-
tures different types of orientation toward action, different types of
confrontation with reality, it serves a useful purpose.

5. "Vorfragen und Grundprobleme der Agudistischen Politik,"
in Jacob Rosenheim, *Agudistische Schriften* (Frankfurt am Main:
Verlag des Israelit und Hermon, 1929), p. 133.

6. See note 5 above, p. 127.

7. See note 5 above. On the disquieting effects of Isaac Breuer's
messianism, cf. Mordechai Breuer, *Jüdische Orthodoxie im
Deutschen Reich*, p. 348.

8. "The halacha itself, the will of God concretized in law, cannot at all be truthfully ascertained without applying general, regulative principles which are derived solely from the divinely willed
developmental goals of the individual and of the society." See note 5
above, p. 121.

9. Quoted in "Zur Organisation der gesetzestreuen Judenheit,"
in Jacob Rosenheim, *Agudistische Schriften*, p. 1.

10. Cited in Provisorischen Comité der Agudas Jisroel, *Agudas
Jisroel: Berichte und Materialien* (Frankfurt am Main: Buro des
Agudas Jisroel, 1912?), p. 11.

11. See note 10 above, frontispiece.

12. For a general overview, cf. Haim Hillel Ben-Sasson, ed., *A
History of the Jewish People* (Cambridge: Harvard University Press,
1976), pp. 847–52.

13. Michael Graetz, "From Corporate Community to Ethnic-
Religious Minority, 1750–1830," LBIYB 37: 1992, p. 76. Amos
Funkenstein, *Perceptions of Jewish History*, pp. 220–34. Allan
Arkush, *Moses Mendelssohn and the Enlightenment*, chap. 7.

14. Cf. Robert Liberles, "Emancipation and the Structure of
the Jewish Community in the Nineteenth Century," LBIYB vol. 31:
1986, pp. 51–67.

15. Michael Graetz, "From Corporate Community to Ethnic-Religious Minority, 1750–1830," pp. 71–72.

16. See note 15 above, pp. 71–82. On the term "orthodoxy," cf. Jacob Katz, "Orthodoxy in Historical Perspective," in Peter Y. Medding, ed., *Studies in Contemporary Jewry*, vol. 2 (Bloomington: Indiana University Press, 1986), p. 4. Katz differentiates between an unreflective tradition-bound Weltanschauung and a conscious option for tradition elected as a response to modernity. Karl Mannheim's notion of conservatism as the deliberate reaction of traditional forces to the disintegrative effects of modernity probably lies behind Prof. Katz's distinction. Cf. Karl Mannheim, "Conservative Thought," in Kurt Wolff, ed., *From Karl Mannheim* (New York: Oxford University Press, 1971). Julius Carlebach, at any rate, (cf. note 21 infra) strenuously objects to Katz's and others' thesis that Orthodoxy is a novel phenomenon in the history of Judaism.

17. S. N. Eisenstadt, "Intellectuals and Tradition," *Daedalus*, Spring 1972, pp. 1–19.

18. Cf. Robert Liberles, *Religious Conflict in Social Context: The Resurgence of Orthodox Judaism in Frankfurt am Main, 1838–1877* (Westport, Greenwood Press, 1985), p. 182 and chap. 7 passim.

19. Cf. Ismar Schorsch, *Jewish Reactions to German Anti-Semitism, 1870–1914* (New York and Philadelphia, Columbia University Press and Jewish Publication Society of America, 1972) and Marjorie Lamberti, *Jewish Activism in Imperial Germany: The Struggle for Civil Equality* (New Haven: Yale University Press, 1978).

20. For the difference between tradition and traditionalism, that is, an ideology of tradition, cf. Jaroslav Pelikan, *The Vindication of Tradition* (New Haven: Yale University Press, 1984).

21. Julius Carlebach, "The Foundations of German-Jewish Orthodoxy, An Interpretation," LBIYB 33:1988, pp. 67–91. Carlebach, like Liberles, argues for the continuity of political culture among the German Jews, including the political functions of the rabbinate, despite the changed circumstances of the emancipatory society. Cf. Steven M. Lowenstein, "Separatist Orthodoxy's Attitudes Toward Community—The Breuer Community in Germany and America," in

Walter P. Zenner, ed., *Persistence and Flexibility: Anthropological Perspectives on the American Jewish Experience* (Albany: State University of New York Press, 1988), p. 209. An interesting reform-oriented commentary on the substantial continuity of German-Jewish communal/political traditions can be found in Ignaz Ziegler, "Die Gemeinde," in *Jüdisches Fest, Jüdischer Brauch: Ein Sammelwerk*, Elsa Rabin and Friedrich Thieberger, eds., (Berlin: Judischer Verlag, 1937), pp. 27–38. (Although printed, the distribution of this anthology was prohibited by the Nazis. The entire text was reissued by the same publisher in 1967.)

22. Jacob Katz's synthetic studies of the early modernization of Ashkenazi Jewry have become well-deserved classics. See: Jacob Katz, *Tradition and Crisis: Jewish Society at the End of the Middle Ages*, Bernard Dov Cooperman, trans. (New York: New York University Press, 1993) and *Out of the Ghetto: The Social Background of Jewish Emancipation 1770–1870* (New York: Schocken Books, 1978).

23. Samson Raphael Hirsch, "Jewish Communal Life," in *Judaism Eternal: Selected Essays from the Writings of Rabbi Samson Raphael Hirsch*, vols. 1, 2. Grunfeld, trans., and ed., (London: Soncino Press, 1956), pp. 97–144.

24. Robert Liberles, *Religious Conflict in Social Context*, passim.

25. Menachem Friedman has argued that the emergence of modern civil society, corellated with the demise of the *kehillah*, allowed Jewish groups to lose those strong ties of mutual obligation which prevailed in the *kehillah*. Without the moderating influence of having to live together in one integrated polity, Jews experienced heightened sectarianism and the rise of extremism in the pursuit of purity and utopian experimentation. Menachem Friedman, "Life Tradition and Book Tradition in the Development of Ultra-Orthodox Judaism," in *Judaism Viewed From Within and Without: Anthropological Studies*, Harvey E. Goldberg, ed., (Albany: State University of New York Press, 1987), pp. 235–55. For a consideration of the same problem from the point of view of phenomenology rather than sociology of religion, cf. Eliezer Goldman, "Responses to Modernity in Orthodox Jewish Thought," in Peter Y. Medding, ed., *Studies in Contemporary Jewry*, vol. 2, esp. pp. 52–55. Note also

Haym Soloveitchik, "Rupture and Reconstruction: The Transformation of Contemporary Orthodoxy," *TRADITION*, vol. 28:4, 1994.

26. Disenchantment and secularization can be analytically distinguished from one another. "Disenchantment" (Weber's *Entzauberung*) refers primarily to the loss of a religious, specifically a sacramental or mystery-bearing worldview. "Secularization" is the broader term, implying not only disenchantment at the level of belief (so called "secularization of consciousness") but also those social and political processes wherein religious institutions retreat from positions of public power and authority and become voluntary, private, or marginalized phenomena. Here, secularization overlaps with aspects of modernization. The distinction between secularization and disenchantment notwithstanding, I shall use these terms more or less interchangeably. For one thing, secularization remains a notoriously vague concept. For another, the processes of intellectual and social transformation are always deeply implicated in one another. The sharper distinction is between disenchantment/secularization and modernization.

27. Hans Gerth and C. Wright Mills, eds., *From Max Weber*, p. 155. For a recent critique of the disenchantment thesis, cf. Ernest Gellner, "The Rubber Cage: Disenchantment with Disenchantment," in his *Culture, Identity and Politics* (London: Cambridge University Press, 1987).

28. Peter Berger drew on Max Weber and traced the modern secularization of the West to the disenchanting orientation of biblical religion. Cf. his *The Sacred Canopy* (New York: Anchor Doubleday, 1967). For the skeptical response of an historian to this sociological thesis, cf. Owen Chadwick, *The Secularization of the European Mind in the Nineteenth Century*, p. 137–39.

29. Cf. infra., Weber, *Ancient Judaism*, p. 4.

30. Freddy Raphael, "Max Weber and Ancient Judaism," in LBIYB, vol. 18, 1973, p. 51. While this statement is certainly overly severe, it does capture some of the underlying orientation of biblical and rabbinic Judaism. Indeed, given the system of commandments, the Bible, the rabbis and their medieval successors, including the mystics, were for the most part unwilling to allow the commandments to be based on divine will and mystery alone. They speculated

on the meaning of the commandments thereby increasing the rationalization of the system, cf. Isaac Heinemann, *The Meaning of the Commandments in the Literature of Israel* (Hebrew) (Jerusalem: Ha-Histadrut Ha-Zionit, 1966) vol. 1.

31. Max Weber, *Economy and Society*, vol. 1, Guenther Roth and Claus Wittich, eds., (Berkeley: University of California Press, 1978), pp. 24–26.

32. Weber's use of the term "traditional" is rather different from our's. Traditionalism in our sense is closer to Weber's *Wertrationalität*, that is, ethically-oriented rational conduct.

33. This is true even regarding kingship for some of the sages (e.g., R. Nehorai in Sifre Devarim 17:156; Midrash Tannaim on Deut. 17:14; and the positions of R. Samuel and R. Jose in T. B. Sanhedrin 20b) and for medieval exegetes such as Don Isaac Abrabanel. For a discussion of rabbinic views regarding whether kingship was mandatory or discretionary see David Polish, "Rabbinic Views on Kingship: A Study in Jewish Sovereignty," *Jewish Political Studies Review* 3:1 and 2, Spring 1991, pp. 67–90.

34. Jacob Z. Lauterbach, trans., *Mekilta de-Rabbi Ishmael*, vol. 2 (Philadelphia: Jewish Publication Society of America, 1976), p. 205. The version of the midrash at Vayikra Rabba 4:6 brings out the organicity of Israel even more forcefully.

35. Yitzhak Baer, "The Origins of Jewish Communal Organization in the Middle Ages," in *Binah*, vol. 1, Joseph Dan, ed., (New York: Praeger, 1989), p. 65.

36. Cf. Shemot Rabba, 25:2, 29:2; Bemidbar Rabba 21:23; Devarim Rabba 2:31 inter alia.

37. So R. Joseph Soloveitchik in *On Repentance* (Hebrew), Pinchas Peli, ed., (Jerusalem: World Zionist Organization, 1974), pp. 93–98. R. Soloveitchik argues that Maimonides requires faith in the reality and efficacy of k'nesset Israel as a component of messianic belief. For the kabbalistic elaboration of k'nesset Israel in its mediating function, cf Alan Mittleman, *Between Kant and Kabbalah* (Albany, State University of New York Press, 1990), p. 169ff.

38. Quoted in Julius Carlebach, "The Foundations of German-Jewish Orthodoxy," LBIYB, vol. 33: 1988, p. 68.

39. Yitzhak Baer, "The Origins of Jewish Communal Organization in the Middle Ages," p. 65. The strongest theory of the "divine right" of the Exilarchate is that of Maimonides who argues that Israel is commanded to appoint an exilarch just as they are commanded (and because they are commanded) to appoint a king. Gerald Blidstein, *Political Principles in Maimonidean Halakha* (Hebrew), p. 46.

40. Gerald Blidstein, "Individual and Community in the Middle Ages: Halakhic Theory," in *Kinship and Consent: The Jewish Political Tradition and its Contemporary Uses*, Daniel J. Elazar, ed., (Lanham, MD: University Press of America, 1983), p. 226.

41. Jacob Z. Lauterbach, trans., *Mekilta de-Rabbi Ishmael*, p. 230.

42. Jon Levenson, *Sinai & Zion: An Entry Into the Jewish Bible* (New York: Harper & Row, 1985), p. 100. Levenson follows Moshe Weinfeld's typology of the "treaty" and the "covenant of grant" to account for the fundamentally different orientations of Sinai and Zion.

43. Covenant is therefore an implicitly ambiguous concept. Insofar as we speak of covenant rather than contract, we affirm a form of social relation in which a transcendent or ontological dimension is crucial. In Jon Levenson's view, the Bible presents two rival versions of covenanting which preserve the ambiguity of orientation toward both the immanent and the transcendent. The traditions associated with the covenant on Mount Sinai present an historical framework for Israelite identity, while the traditions of the Davidic covenant of Zion present a cosmic/primordial identity. (Cf. note 42 above, pp. 41, 155.) Thus, while these different traditions of covenanting and of the self-representations of the Jewish polity which are affiliated with them can be differentiated for analytical purposes, we should not expect to find pure instances of them in post-biblical Jewish thought. Sometimes one filiation of the tradition is favored, sometimes the other. Often in midrash, and especially in Jehuda Halevi, the Zohar and kabbala generally, the organic view prevails. Jews are different from non-Jews in a metaphysical way. They are essentially different; they have a different kind of soul; a different kind of nature. Israel is not just "one people, unique in all the world"; it is ontologically unique: unique in all possible worlds. Jewish being

per se is *enchanted*. For another stream of the tradition, typified by philosophical rationalists such as Maimonides, Jews and non-Jews are separated by belief alone. (Cf. Menachem Kellner, *Maimonides on Judaism and the Jewish People* (Albany: State University of New York Press, 1991), pp. 1–7. Cf. Jacob Katz, *Tradition and Crisis*, pp. 23–25.) They actualize their human natures in discrepant, indeed, in inferior and superior ways, but their natures reflect a single human substance. Jews, Judaism, and Jewish community can become *disenchanted* when they fail to conform to the Torah.

44. Yitzhak Baer,"The Origins of Jewish Communal Organization in the Middle Ages," p. 63. Cf. Ignaz Ziegler, "Die Gemeinde," in Elsa Rabin and Friedrich Thieberger, *Jüdisches Fest, Jüdischer Brauch*.

45. Sanhedrin 14b, Rosh Hashana 25b, cf. Baruch Ha-Levy Epstein, *Torah Temima* (New York: Hebrew Publishing Co., 1928) Deut. 17:9 ad loc.

46. Cf. the discussion in Gerald Blidstein, "Notes on Hefker Bet Din in Talmudic and Medieval Law," *Dine Israel* 4, (1973), pp. 35–49 and Gerald Blidstein, "Individual and Community in the Middle Ages: Halakhic Theory," pp. 216, 220, 223.

47. Louis Finkelstein, *Jewish Self-Government in the Middle Ages* (Westport, CT: Greenwood Press Publishers, 1975), pp. 6–10.

48. On the rabbis' role in validating communal authority in both a foundational and an ongoing way cf. Menachem Elon, *Jewish Law*, vol. 2, p. 684ff.

49. Karl Mannheim, *Ideology and Utopia*, p. 113

50. Cf. the illuminating discussion of Shalom Albeck in his *The Law of Property and Contract in the Talmud* (Hebrew), (Tel Aviv: Dvir Publishers, 1976), pp. 506–16. Albeck argues consistently for a contractarian, consensual basis for the authority of the community. He rejects the analogy of the community to a court as a later retrojection on the talmudic material. In his view, political obligation or communal coercion is legitimated by an implicit compact the individual has made with the majority of residents based on the obvious benefits of social life. Albeck understands the talmudic materials to assimilate citizenship to the legal paradigm of partnership, particularly of economic partnership where the element of

rational calculation in the pursuit of gain is prominent. Albeck has thus embedded politics in an halakhic framework (*shutafut*) without recourse to the court model. His model preserves a maximal dimension of freedom of decision and discretion for the political actors.

Menachem Elon, on the other hand, rejects the sufficiency of *shutafut* as a model for public authority, claiming that it illicitly analogizes public affairs to private affairs. He finds a categorical distinction between the two, based on the element of compulsion which characterizes public law. He therefore regards the court model as a more authoritative and powerful conceptual system. Additionally, he claims that the court model prevailed historically because it allowed for, among other things, greater creativity and authority in public decision making than the partnership model. Elon is saying, therefore, that the inner tendency of the court model is toward what I am calling politics rather than toward administration. Cf. Menachem Elon, "Power and Authority: Halakhic Stance of the Traditional Community and its Contemporary Implications," in *Kinship and Consent*, Daniel J. Elazar, ed., pp. 186, 199–202. Cf. also his *Jewish Law*, vol. 2, p. 681.

My view is that there always remains a tension between administrative and political impulses. This tension expresses itself within both models: the court model is pushed to the limit to provide for creative, political action and the partnership model is constructed so as to establish stability and organic order, as we shall see in the case of Rabbenu Tam.

51. R. Isaac b. Sheshet Perfet (Ribash) a fourteenth century Spanish authority disputed the necessity for oversight altogether, except in the case of tradesmen. Elon, *Jewish Law*, vol. 2, p. 754. For a schematic overview of the powers of community boards as delegated by Jewish law, cf. Israel Schepansky, *The Takkanot of Israel*, vol. 4, pp. 54–77.

52. Gerald Blidstein, "Individual and Community in the Middle Ages: Halakhic Theory," p. 223. Blidstein also points out, in his essay on the discretionary powers of communal authorities, that the sages of the Talmud saw the need for discretion, that is, promulgating *takkanot* as occasional and extraordinary. This reflects their, in our terms, administrative bent. Medievals such as Maimonides and R. Nissim of Gerona (Ran), by contrast, expand discretionary power to the extent that it serves as the basis of their theories of government. Cf. Blidstein, "Ideal and Real," p. 47.

53. See note 52 above, p. 217. For the institutionalization of this principle, cf. Jacob Katz, *Tradition and Crisis*, p. 73.

54. See note 52 above, p. 227.

55. Tosefta Sanhedrin 2.13. Majority rule received an authoritative formulation in the *takkanot* of Rabbenu Gershom, cf. Finkelstein, *Jewish Self-Government in the Middle Ages*, pp. 33, 121.

56. See note 55 above, Finkelstein, p. 49.

57. See note 55 above, Finkelstein, p. 50, cf. note 52 above, pp. 237–39.

58. See note 55 above, Finkelstein, p. 55.

59. See note 22 above, pp. 73–74.

60. See note 22 above, p. 71.

61. See note 22 above, pp. 67, 72–75.

62. See note 22 above, p. 70.

63. See note 22 above, p. 74.

64. See note 22 above, p. 75.

65. See note 22 above, pp. 198–99.

66. See note 22 above, p. 198. On the gentile legitimation of Jewish power, cf. Robert Chazan, "Medieval Jewish Political Institutions: Foundations of their Authority," in Zvi Gitelman, ed., *The Quest for Utopia*, p. 68. For a detailed study of the rise and decline of the supra-kehillot organizations of Eastern Europe in conjunction with government policies, cf. Eli Lederhendler, *The Road to Modern Jewish Politics: Political Tradition and Political Reconstruction in Tsarist Russia* (New York: Oxford University Press, 1989) pp. 11–57.

67. See note 22 above, p. 77.

68. See note 22 above, p. 78.

69. For an overview of the contents of the Frankfurt takanot, cf. M. Nadav, "Pinkas Kahal Frankfurt d'Main," *Kiryat Sefer*, vol. 31

(Jerusalem: Magnes Press, 1955–1956), pp. 507–16. For an analysis of the communal constitution in the seventeenth and eighteenth centuries, cf. Isadore Kracauer, *Geschichte der Juden in Frankfurt A.M.*, vol. 2 (Frankfurt A.M.: Vorstand der Israelitischen Gemeinde Frankfurt a.M., 1927), pp. 178–85. Additional comments on Frankfurt, especially concerning the extent to which "laymen" were empowered in its community constitution may be found in Israel Schepansky, *The Takkanot of Israel*, vol. 4, p. 228.

70. Robert Liberles, *Religious Conflict in Social Context*, ch. 3, p. 87ff.

71. Menachem Friedman, "Life Tradition and Book Tradition," in Harvey Goldberg, ed., *Judaism Viewed From Within and Without*.

72. See note 70 above, p. 164.

73. For a typology and analysis of utopian mentalities, cf. Karl Mannheim, *Ideology and Utopia*, chap. 4, especially pp. 219–39. It seems to me possible to combine Mannheim's categories without a loss of intelligibility, since they are intended as ideal types and any approximation to reality will require adjustment. Hirsch and his followers partook of the optimism and progressivism of a liberal, rationalistic age. On the other hand, their task was restorative rather than progressive.

74. By stressing the overall rationality of Hirsch's approach, I do not mean to imply that he lacked warmth or feeling toward the tradition. On the contrary, his writings are animated by passionate attachment to the realia and riches of the tradition, including, to some degree, the mystical tradition. Hirsch appeals to will and feeling as much as and perhaps more than he appeals to reason. At any rate, by rationality I mean to refer not to the philosophical character of his thought but to its sociological significance. It is oriented toward shaping and sustaining a well-thought out communal reality governed by clear ideas. Hirsch epitomizes Weberian ethical rationality. On Hirsch's relation to mysticism, n.b. Mordechai Breuer, *Jüdische Orthodoxie im Deutschen Reich, 1871–1918*, p. 72.

75. Samson Raphael Hirsch, "Jewish Communal Life," in *Judaism Eternal*, vol. 2, Isadore Grunfeld, trans. and ed., (London: Soncino Press, 1956) p. 103. Jacob Rosenheim concurred that the Torah is Israel's sole sovereign. In his speech before the newly con-

stituted Central Committee of Agudah, he writes that Agudah recognizes the Torah "as the sole sovereign of the Jewish people" (*als einzigen Souveräns des jüdischen Volkes*). Its goal is to establish the "lordship of the Torah in klal Israel" (*Herrschaft der Thora in Klall Jisroel*). Rosenheim cites Deut. 33:5 to indicate that the messianic time in which God will be king is approaching, as the "tribes of Israel" organize in the Agudah. *Blätter*, vol. 7, no. 18, April 7, 1921.

76. All references are taken from the standard collection of medieval exegesis, *Mikraot Gedolot* (Jerusalem: Pardes, n.d.) Deut. 33:4–5 ad loc.

77. On the role of *Bildung* in shaping the German-Jewish identity, cf. David Sorkin, *The Transformation of German Jewry, 1780–1840* (New York: Oxford University Press, 1987). For a nuanced discussion of Hirsch's educational philosophy, cf. Mordechai Breuer, *Jüdische Orthodoxie im Deutschen Reich, 1871–1918*, pp. 73–82.

78. See note 23 above, p. 120ff.

79. See note 23 above, p. 119.

80. See note 23 above, p. 124.

81. See note 23 above, p. 132–33.

82. See note 23 above, p. 116.

83. See note 23 above, p. 110. For the importance of laity in the resurgence of Frankfurt Orthodoxy through founding Talmud study Vereine and, in general, organising the Religionsgesellschaft, cf. Robert Liberles, *Religious Conflict in Social Context*, p. 156.

84. See note 23 above, p. 134.

85. Gershon Bacon, "Haredi Conceptions of Obligations and Rights," pp. 85–95.

86. See note 23 above, p. 103.

87. Cf. for example, the discussion in Stephan Eisel, *Minimalkonsens und freiheitliche Demokratie* (Paderborn: Schöningh, 1986), pp. 36–38. The ambivalence of this maximalist concept toward a free and pluralistic society in the modern liberal

sense is also found in Hirsch. Hirsch appealed to the State to grant his community the right to separate on the modernist grounds of freedom of religion. The freedom to practice one's religion independent of state or social coercion does not necessarily mean, however, that the religion so practiced comports with the values of liberal individualism. For a discussion of different conceptions of freedom and democracy vis a vis Jewish communal thought cf., Alan Mittleman, "From Private Rights to Public Good," *Jewish Political Studies Review* 5:1–2, (Spring 1993), pp. 79–93.

88. Numbers Rabbah, Parshat Beha'alothecha, 15:18. Soncino Translation, p. 662. Another famous midrash which takes up this theme (Leviticus Rabbah, Parshat Emor, 30:12) describes the different characteristics of the four species of plant that are tied together to form the palm branch and citron used ritualistically on Sukkot. Analogizing each of these species to different kinds of Jewish personality, the midrash asks what use God can make of this composite people:
"What then does the Holy One, blessed be He. do to them? To destroy them is impossible. But, says the Holy One, blessed be He, let them all be tied together in one band so (says God), then at that instant I am exalted. Hence it is written, "It is He that buildeth His upper chambers in the heaven." (Amos 9:6) When is he exalted? What time they are made into band: as it says, "When He hath founded His band upon the earth."
Nachmanides also calls attention to the use of the term agudah in the Rosh Hashana liturgy where Israel, striving to be an *agudah ahat*, proclaims the sovereignty of God with the blasts of the shofar. The familiar and dramatic use of this phrase in the New Year liturgy influenced, no doubt, its selection as the name of the organization.

89. "Die Agudistische Einheitsgedanke," in *Agudistische Schriften*, Jacob Rosenheim (Frankfurt am Main: Verlag des Israelit und Hermon, 1930), p. 151. The essays on Agudat Israel, many originally published in Rosenheim's newspaper, *Der Israelit*, were also published as part five, volume two of Rosenheim's two volume collection, *Ohale Jacob: Ausgewählte Aufsätze und Ansprachen* (Frankfurt am Main: J. Kauffmann Verlag, 1930), pp. 159–320 (=AAA). All references here will be to the separate fascicle.

90. See note 89 above, "Die Agudistische Einheitsgedanke," p. 152.

91. Ibid., p. 153.

92. For analysis of Adolf Buechner and his teaching, cf. Owen Chadwick, *The Secularization of the European Mind in the Nineteenth Century*. Rosenheim, ibid., p. 154.

93. Rosenheim, ibid., p. 157.

94. The Jewish people is described as the "Kunderin des kosmischen und geschichtlichen Einheitsgedankens." Ibid., p. 158.

95. Ibid., p. 159.

96. Ibid., p. 160. The source for Rosenheim's closing citation: *Shutafim l'kadosh barukh hu b'maaseh vereishit* is B. Shabbat 10a. Talmudic citation asserts that righteous judges participate with God in the work of creation. Rosenheim thereby ascribes a cosmological significance to the work of Agudat Israel.

97. Cf. Karl Mannheim, "Conservative Thought," in Kurt Wolff, ed., *From Karl Mannheim*, pp. 165, 171, 176.

CHAPTER 3

1. Isaac Breuer, *Mein Weg* (Zurich: Morascha Verlag, 1988), p. 16.

2. For a general overview of early modern Jewish organizational activity cf. Daniel J. Elazar, *People and Polity: The Organizational Dynamics of World Jewry* (Detroit: Wayne State University Press, 1989). Note also H. H. Ben-Sasson, ed., *A History of the Jewish People* (Cambridge: Harvard University Press, 1976), chap. 53.

3. Robert Liberles, "Emancipation and the Structure of the Jewish Community in the Nineteenth Century," LBIYB 31:1986, pp. 51–67.

4. Amos Funkenstein has argued that the terms "emancipation," "assimilation" and "integration," were routinely confused in popular Jewish discourse. Contemporary Jews believed that emancipation could only be achieved through assimilation which would then result in integration. In the political theories of certain intellectuals, however, the concepts were properly differentiated. Jews assumed, for reasons that seemed powerfully persuasive at the time

(not least among them, gentile demands) that emancipation would come about as a consequence of cultural assimilation. Such assimilation in turn would result in full-fledged social integration, the social counterpart to legal equality of rights. Funkenstein argues that only Mendelssohn, Marx and Herzl were able to separate these terms. Mendelssohn pled for emancipation without thoroughgoing assimilation. Marx saw no reason for Jews to assimilate, that is, shed their alleged essentially mendacious character in order to achieve emancipation, because emancipation in the bourgeois sense is illusory anyway. Herzl analysed the failure of emancipation and assimilation to effect integration and called for national auto-emancipation as the solution to Europe's (and the Jews') Jewish problem. Liberles's analysis affords one an opportunity to question the extent to which Funkenstein has drawn the contrast between his three thinkers and the Jewish masses. The transformation and flourishing of Jewish organizational life at the popular and elite, but nonintellectual, levels circumscribes the assimilatory tendencies of nineteenth century Jewries. It attests, at a popular level, to a continuity of political tradition and consciousness, that is, to a practical, implied differentiation between emancipation and assimilation. Cf. Amos Funkenstein, *Perceptions of Jewish History*, (Berkeley: University of California Press, 1993), pp. 221–34. On the history of the term "emancipation" as such, cf. Jacob Katz, "The Term "Jewish Emancipation": Its Origin and Historical Impact," in Alexander Altmann, ed., *Studies in Nineteenth Century Jewish Intellectual History* (Cambridge: Harvard University Press, 1964).

5. See note 3 above, pp. 53–56.

6. H. H. Ben-Sasson, ed., *A History of the Jewish People*, p. 850.

7. Cf., S. N. Eisenstadt, "Intellectuals and Tradition," *Daedalus*, Spring 1972, pp. 1–19; and especially "Post-traditional Societies and the Continuation and Reconstruction of Tradition," *Daedalus*, Winter 1973, pp. 1–27. Eisenstadt's model of selective appropriation and subsequent transformation of traditional institutional structures well accords with the historical data assembled and analyzed by Liberles.

8. See note 3 above, p. 63. Marjorie Lamberti, *Jewish Activism in Imperial Germany* (New Haven: Yale University Press, 1978), pp.

2–6. Ismar Schorsch, *Jewish Reactions to German Anti-Semitism, 1870–1914* (New York and Philadelphia: Columbia University Press and Jewish Publication Society of America, 1972), pp. 18–21, 75. Strong traditions of localism among German Jews go back to the middle ages. The takkanot of a Frankfurt synod in 1603, restrict the authority of rabbis to their own locales. Cf. Israel Schepansky, *The Takkanot of Israel*, vol. 4, p. 228.

9. See note 3 above, pp. 2–6.

10. Extreme Jewish assimilationists believed that even the local state-recognized community was a barrier to full assimilation. Cf. Uriel Tal, *Christians and Jews in Germany: Religion, Politics and Ideology in the Second Reich, 1870–1914*, Noah Jonathan Jacobs, trans., (Ithaca: Cornell University Press, 1975), p. 59.

11. See note 8 above, Schorsch, chap. 1.

12. Cf. Jacob Toury, *Die politischen Orientierungen der Juden in Deutschland* (Tübingen: J. C. B. Mohr [Paul Siebeck], 1966) especially section C, and Marjorie Lamberti, *Jewish Activism in Imperial Germany* (New Haven: Yale University Press, 1978). Liberals and Progressives were the main force behind the creation of the Verein zur Abwehr des Antisemitismus (1891), a largely Christian organization which propagandized against the virulent racialist anti-Semitism of the 1890s. They conceived of anti-Semitism less as a Jewish problem than as a national problem. Cf. note 11 above, chap. 3.

13. See note 10 above, Tal, cf. esp. chap. 1.

14. Yaakov Tsur, *German Jewish Orthodoxy and its Attitude Toward Internal Organization and Zionism, 1896–1911* (Hebrew), (Diss., Tel Aviv University, 1982), p. 1.

15. See note 8 above, Lamberti, pp. 8–9.

16. See note 15 above, pp. 9–22; see note 8 above, Schorsch, chaps. 4, 5.

17. See note 14 above, p. 7.

18. See note 11 above, pp. 204ff.

19. See note 11 above, p. 130, note 25.

20. See note 11 above, p. 77.

21. For the history of the FV before 1903, cf. the work of its first executive director, Samson Raphael Hirsch's son, N. Hirsch, *Die Freie Vereinigung für die Interessen des orthodoxen Judentums: eine Beleuchtung ihrer Aufgabe und seitherigen Wirksamkeit* (Frankfurt am Main: Louis Golde, 1903). For general background cf. also Joseph Carlebach, *Das Gesetztreue Judentum*, p. 44. (Carlebach gives an incorrect date [1878], also for the founding of Agudat Israel [1913, p. 46].); Hermann Schwab, *The History of Orthodox Jewry in Germany*, pp. 89, 101–03 and chap. 14 passim; Yehuda Ben Avner, *Vom Orthodoxen Judentum in Deutschland zwischen Zwei Weltkriegen*, p. 8; Mordechai Breuer, *Jüdische Orthodoxie im Deutschen Reich*, pp. 248–49; see note 14 above, chap. 5.

22. The text of Hirsch's call to action is in Naphtali Hirsch, *Die Freie Vereinigung*, p. 4.

23. For the role of the havurah in antiquity, cf. Jacob Neusner, ed., *Contemporary Judaic Fellowship in Theory and Practice* (New York: Ktav, 1972), esp. part 1. For havurot as mediating institutions vis a vis the medieval *kehillah*, cf. Jacob Katz, *Tradition and Crisis*, chap. 16.

24. The fact that the medieval havurah was a subsidiary body of the *kehillah* was not acknowledged by Hirsch. He construes the havurah as a supra-communal structure. Hence, his appeal to past precedents, while necessary to his argument, is rather forced.

25. Naphtali Hirsch, *Die Freie Vereinigung*, pp. 18–19. Herman Schwab, *The History of Orthodox Jewry in Germany*, chap. 14. Ismar Schorsch, *Jewish Reactions to German Anti-Semitism*, pp. 33–34, 75–77, 153. Jacob Rosenheim, *Erinnerungen, 1870–1920*, (Frankfurt am Main: Waldemar Kramer Verlag, 1970), pp. 79–81.

26. On Hirsch's singular sense of mission cf. Robert Liberles, *Religious Conflict in Social Context*, pp. 126–33. Hirsch often saw and portrayed himself as an Elijah-like figure, absolutely alone against an army of false prophets. In the present text, the Orthodox per se are so construed. On the self-consciousness of the Orthodox as the Jewish elite, cf. Mordechai Breuer, *Jüdische Orthodoxie im Deutschen Reich*, pp. 44–45.

27. See note 25 above, Hirsch, pp. 11–19.

28. *Statuten der freien Vereinigung für die Interessen des ortho-doxen Judentums* (Frankfurt am Main: M. Slobotsky, 1886), p. 4. Wiener Library (Tel Aviv) Wie7:FRE. The term *Glaubensgenossen* is from Hirsch's call and is not found in the Statutes.

29. See note 28 above, pp. 7–10.

30. See note 28 above, p. 90.

31. See note 28 above, p. 88.

32. Yaakov Tsur, *German Jewish Orthodoxy and its Attitude Toward Internal Organization and Zionism*, p. 8.

33. See note 25 above, Rosenheim, p. 82.

34. For a geographical overview of the communities and a description of their different types of constitution, cf. Joseph Carlebach, *Das Gesetztreue Judentum*, pp. 52–53.

35. See note 11 above, Schorsch, pp. 150ff; see note 25 above, Rosenheim, pp. 78–79.

36. Rosenheim, ibid.

37. Rosenheim, AAA, vol. 2, p. 19.

38. Cf. Karl Mannheim, *Ideology and Utopia*, chap. 4.

39. The concrete form and tasks of the FV are outlined by Rosenheim in his 1907 proposal, reprinted as a portion of "Der Zusammenschluss der deutschen Orthodoxie," in AAA, vol. 2, pp. 21–23.

40. See note 25 above, Rosenheim, p. 85.

41. See note 25 above, Rosenheim, p. 87. For an appreciative biography of R. Marcus/Mordechai Horowitz and an exposition of his point of view, cf. Isaac Unna, "Rabbi Dr. Mordechai Halevi Horowitz: His Life and Work," in Mordechai Horowitz, *Frankfurter Rabbis* (Hebrew), (Jerusalem: Mossad Harav Kook, 1972), pp. 329–41.

42. Rosenheim, ibid., cf. note 1 above, pp. 16–21. Isaac Breuer insists that the boycott was never directed toward persons as such. One could have civil, honorable relations with individuals without regard to which group they belonged. The boycott was directed solely

against the institutions of the general Jewish community. In this sense, Jacob Rosenheim's use of the term *herem* is quite inexact. That one could not discriminate against persons in the sense of a herem is clear from the fact that leading members of the Austrittsgemeinde, including, for example, Rosenheim's father, did not separate either in 1876 or much later from the main Gemeinde.

43. See note 1 above, pp. 31–33. Cf. also his *Moriah* (Hebrew), (Jerusalem: Ha-Sifriya l'ma'an Sifrut Haredit ba-Eretz Yisrael, 1954) pp. 3–18.

44. Much of Rosenheim's attitude is revealed in the following: "Indeed, the Religionsgesellschaft had never really been a genuine Austrittsgemeinde. And just as men like Louis Feist, who, despite belonging to the circle of Marcus Horowitz, became the *rosh ha-kahal* (the President), so too could, in increasing numbers, other honest, religious Yehudim have been won for the Orthodox cause." Rosenheim points out that leading members and families of the IRG had not completely severed their ties with the main community. In terms of our analysis, periphery and center, profane and sacred are already mutually implicated in Rosenheim's thought. The sacred does not and cannot exist in isolation. Cf. note 25 above, Rosenheim, p. 87. Cf. also "Agudas Jisroel als Aufgabe und Verwirklichung," in *Agudistische Schriften*, p. 74, where Rosenheim explicitly states that center and periphery depend on one another.

45. See note 25 above, Rosenheim, p. 88. For a comprehensive overview of the FV's activities during the first decade of the twentieth century, cf. ibid., pp. 89–102. For a description of liberal Jewish initiatives which Rosenheim and the FV opposed during the same period, cf. note 8 above, Lamberti, pp. 137–156, esp. pp. 147–49.

46. See note 25 above, Rosenheim, p. 90.

47. See note 25 above, Rosenheim, pp. 88–93.

48. Theodor Herzl, *The Jewish State* (New York: American Zionist Emergency Council, 1946), p. 138. On the theory of the *gestor negotiorum*, cf. Amos Funkenstein, *Perceptions of Jewish History*, p. 233.

49. See Michael Berkowitz, *Zionist Culture and West European Jewry before the First World War* (Cambridge: Cambridge University Press, 1993), ch. 1.

50. On Halevy, generally see Asher Reichel, *The Letters of Rabbi Isaac Halevy* (Hebrew), (Jerusalem: Mossad Harav Kook, 1972); Hermann Schwab, *The History of Orthodox Jewry in Germany*, pp. 112, 115, 119; on Halevy's scholarship and his impact on Orthodox thought and letters, cf. Mordechai Breuer, *Jüdische Orthodoxie im Deutschen Reich*, pp. 178–185. Cf. note 14 above, pp. 388–95.

51. See note 50 above, Reichel, p. 50.

52. See note 50 above, Reichel, letter 59, p. 131.

53. See note 50 above, Reichel, letters 85–86, pp. 157–58. In letter 85, Halevy writes to Kottek that his proposal for an expanded Palestine Commission, under the name Agudat Israel, will be on the agenda for that Commission's November, 1908 meeting, but that he personally cannot attend. He fears that if he is not present, the matter will die in committee and pleads with Kottek to go and represent him. Apparently, the issue was raised in the commission and a decision was taken to proceed with founding a new organization. Tsur claims that Halevy took too much credit for the Agudah idea and that Rosenheim wanted to develop an international Orthodox organization, with a strong focus on Palestine, before Halevy prodded him in that direction. It seems to me that Rosenheim may have spoken rather rhetorically about this, but that he still saw a developed FV as the most practical way of realizing his organizational ends. Cf. note 14 above, p. 389.

54. See note 50 above, Reichel, p. 158. Cf. note 25 above, Rosenheim, p. 111. Although both Rosenheim and Breuer were hesitant to appear too "Palestinocentric," Rosenheim was more inclined to stress Zionist-like concerns than was Breuer. It is ironic that Breuer's son, Isaac Breuer, should have later been so relentlessly critical of Rosenheim for his alleged lack of appreciation of the conceptual and political centrality of Palestine. Cf. note 14 above, p. 390.

55. Rosenheim's reluctance to create an entirely new, international organization rather than an expanded FV may have been due to his desire to retain German Jewish control over the organization. Halevy, by contrast, favored a new organization so that Eastern European Jewry would have a predominant position. Tsur, ibid., p. 390.

56. See note 25 above, Rosenheim, p. 112. The proposal to meet in Bad Homburg was apparently Halevy's, cf. note 50 above, Reichel, p. 58. It was primarily on the basis of Halevy's credibility and friendship with some of the Lithuanian rabbis that they participated in the deliberations. Halevy allayed their fears that the Agudah would promote the penetration of German secular culture (i.e., *Bildung* or Hirsch's "torah im derekh eretz") in the east. For Rosenheim's own responsiveness to this anxiety, cf. note 25 above, Rosenheim, p. 122. For a contemporary example of what the Easterners feared, cf. Hermann Cohen's proposal for redesigning eastern yeshivot on the model of the German "scientific" rabbinical school: Hermann Cohen, "Der polnische Jude," in *Jüdische Schriften*, Bruno Strauss, ed., (Berlin: C. A. Schwetschke & Sohn, 1924) vol. 2, pp. 166–67.

57. In support of the Agudist view, Halevy invokes the statement of the Zohar, "The Holy Blessed be He, the Torah and Israel are one." (Zohar, Ahare Mot, chap. 63) as support for his organic point of view. See note 50 above, Reichel, p. 60 and letter 105, p. 172.

58. Adolf Weyl, "Die Vorgeschichte der Agudas Jisroel," in *Agudas Jisroel: Berichte und Materialien*, p. 6.

59. See note 25 above, Rosenheim, p. 114.

60. See note 58 above, p. 7.

61. See note 25 above, Rosenheim p. 115.

62. On the distinction between contractual and organic conceptions of Jewish peoplehood, cf. note 25 above, Rosenheim, pp. 75–79.

63. See note 50 above, Reichel, p. 175.

64. See note 49 above, Berkowitz, esp. ch. 2; Ben Halpern, *The Idea of the Jewish State*, p. 85. For the history of Misrachi's prior difficulties with the *Kulturfrage*, cf. Ehud Luz, *Parallels Meet: Religion and Nationalism in the Early Zionist Movement, 1882–1904*, Lenn Schramm, trans., (Philadelphia: Jewish Publication Society, 1988), pp. 241–46. Cf. also David Vital, *Zionism: The Crucial Phase* (Oxford: Oxford University Press, 1987), pp. 56–57.

65. See note 58 above, p. 8. Significantly, Adolf Weyl, a teacher at the IRG's Realschule, was one of the Mizrachists who left to join the provisional committee. Also, see note 25 above, Rosenheim, pp. 115–117.

66. See note 33 above, Rosenheim, p. 117.

67. See note 33 above, Rosenheim, p. 118.

68. See note 58 above, pp. 14–15.

69. See note 14 above, p. 390.

70. Compare the claim of Herr Braun of Frankfurt that the organization, if it is to exist at all must exist as a "union of klal Israel." "The new organization should be a corrective to the Jewish history of the last century." See note 58 above, p. 20.

71. See note 58 above, pp. 16, 18.

72. See note 58 above, p. 23.

73. See note 58 above.

74. See note 58 above, p. 99.

75. In Daniel Elazar's terminology, this constitutes a "ketaric" conflict, that is, a conflict of interest between the *keter malkhut*, the lay elite, and the *keter torah*, the authoritative interpreters of Torah.

76. See note 58 above, pp. 71–100.

77. See note 25 above, Rosenheim, p. 123.

78. See note 58 above, p. 72.

79. Y. Tsvi Zahavy, *From the Hatam Sofer to Herzl* (Hebrew). (Jerusalem: The Zionist Library of the Zionist Organization, 1972), pp. 190–95.

80. See note 25 above, Rosenheim, p. 129.

81. Cf. the views of the president of the British Orthodox rabbinate, R. Daiches. See note 58 above, p. 76.

82. Cf. for example, the view of the Viennese leader, R. Furst. See note 58 above, p. 80.

83. See note 58 above, p. 93.

84. See note 58 above, p. 96.

85. See note 25 above, Rosenheim, p. 124.

86. See note 25 above, Rosenheim, pp. 130–31. Rosenheim points out, in evident pain, that many in the IRG treated the "uncultivated Polacks" with, at best, paternalistic condescension. On the negativism or ambivalence of the German Orthodox toward the Ostjuden cf. *Unwanted Strangers*, Jack Wertheimer (New York: Oxford University Press, 1987), pp. 172–73; and Stephen Aschheim, *Brothers and Strangers* (Madison: University of Wisconsin Press, 1982).

87. See note 25 above, Rosenheim, p. 130.

88. Rosenheim relates in his memoirs (ibid., p. 130) that Breuer was prepared to view non-separatist Orthodox Jews as those who "divide themselves from the community," (*porshim min ha-tsibbur*) but not as those who "divide themselves from the ways of the community" (*porshim mi-darkhei tsibbur*). The first phrase derives from a statement of Hillel's in Pirke Avot 2:4, "Do not divide yourself from the community, nor trust yourself until the day of your death, nor judge another until you stand in his place." It is found in the Talmud, B. T. Taanit 11a in a discussion of persons who fast improperly or not at all during periods of communal fasting. They who do not share in the community's woes, we are told, will not experience the community's redemption. (Cf. Shulkhan Arukh, Orekh Hayyim, 574:5) The term poresh mi-darkhei tsibbur, by contrast, comes from B. T. Rosh Hashanah 17a where it signifies a category of completely wicked person who will not inherit the world to come. (Cf. Mishneh Torah, Laws of Repentance, Ch. 3:11 for Maimonides's precise explication of the term.) The former term therefore signifies a "normal" sort of sin, the latter a more heinous sin. Breuer declined to consider Orthodox non-members of his community as extreme sinners in this sense.

89. See note 25 above, Rosenheim, p. 130.

90. Jacob Rosenheim, "Die Hungarische Forderung und die Verfassung der Agudas Jisroel," in *Agudistische Schriften* (Frankfurt am Main: Verlag des Israelit und Hermon, n.d.), p. 17. The article originally appeared during November, 1912 in Israelit.

91. See note 90 above, p. 17.

92. See note 90 above, p. 20. Rosenheim appears to be following the Talmudic principle requiring legislators to realistically consider

what the public is able to abide by when they draft their legislation, for example, Baba Kamma 79b.

93. See note 25 above, Rosenheim, p. 138.

94. "Provisorisches Organisations-Statut fur den Gruppenverband der Agudas Jisroel in Deutschland," para. 2. The German Landesorganisation (or "Gruppenverband") adopted this provisional statute at Halberstadt on December 15, 1913. The German and Swiss groups were the first national chapters developed. The German organization was located in Halberstadt in order to avoid the persistent division of Orthodoxy in Frankfurt. (A copy of this document is in the archive of the Jewish Museum of Frankfurt.)

95. The activities of Agudat Israel during and shortly after the First World War are chronicled in Rosenheim, *Erinnerungen*, pp. 140–59; and Rosenheim, *Agudistische Schriften*, pp. 168–72.

96. Verfassung der Agudas Jisroel-Weltorganisation, section 1, para. 3, in Rosenheim, *Agudistische Schriften*, p. 164.

97. See note 96 above, section 2, para. 4, in Rosenheim, ibid.

98. See note 1 above, p. 32.

99. See note 1 above, p. 31.

100. Isaac Breuer, *Messiasspuren* (Frankfurt am Main: Verlag Rudolph Leonhard Hammon, 1918), passim.

101. See Rosenheim, "Vorfragen und Grundprobleme der Agudistischen Politik," *Agudistische Schriften*, p. 128.

102. Interestingly, the name Agudat Israel, which was associated strongly with Germany, was not used in order to not antagonize delegates from the victorious Allied countries. Although Rosenheim used the name in his speech, the meeting was officially designated "Weltkonferenz der juedisch-orthodox Verbände" (World Conference of Jewish Orthodox Societies). The conference established the new headquarters of the movement in neutral Switzerland. It soon moved to Vienna however.

103. See Rosenheim, "Agudas Jisroel als Weltorganisation," in *Agudistische Schriften*, p. 31.

104. See note 103 above, pp. 32–33.

105. See note 103 above, p. 35.

106. See note 103 above, p. 37.

107. God's *kavod* (sacred presence) is tangible in His creation (*malkhuto; kavod malkhuto*). Cf. Rosenheim, "Agudas Israel als Aufgabe und Verwirklichung," *Agudistische Schriften*, pp. 59–61.

108. See note 107 above, pp. 64–71.

109. See the address by Wolf Jacobson, "15 Jahre Agudas Jisroel," in *Korrespondenzblatt der Agudas-Jisroel-Jugendorganisation*, vol. 2, no. 4, Frankfurt am Main, April 1927. (Wiener Library, Tel Aviv, W 477) Jacobson tries to reconcile the realities of political life with a Rosenheim-inspired metahistorical conception of the organization.

110. See note 109 above, p. 7.

BIBLIOGRAPHY

Agudas Jisroel: Berichte und Materialien. Frankfurt am Main: Provisorischen Comite der "Agudas Jisroel," 1912(?).

Albeck, Shalom. *Dinei Mammonot b'Talmud* [The Law of Property and Contract in the Talmud]. Tel Aviv: Dvir Publishers, 1976.

Altmann, Alexander. *Studies in Nineteenth Century Jewish Intellectual History*. Cambridge: Harvard University Press, 1964.

Arkush, Allan. *Moses Mendelssohn and the Enlightenment*. Albany: State University of New York Press, 1994.

Aschheim, Stephen. *Brothers and Strangers*. Madison: University of Wisconsin Press, 1982.

Bacon, Gershon. "Agudath Israel in Poland, 1916–1939: An Orthodox Response to the Challenge of Modernity." Ph.D. diss. Columbia University, 1979.

Baron, Salo. *The Jewish Community*, 3 vols. Philadelphia: Jewish Publication Society of America, 1948.

Ben Avner, Yehuda. *Vom Orthodoxen Judentum in Deutschland zwischen Zwei Weltkriegen*. Hildesheim: Georg Olms Verlag, 1987.

Ben-Sasson, H. H. and S. Ettinger, eds. *Jewish Society Throughout the Ages*. New York: Schocken Books, 1973.

Berger, Peter. *The Sacred Canopy*. New York: Anchor Doubleday, 1967.

Berkowitz, Michael. *Zionist Culture and West European Jewry before the First World War*. Cambridge: Cambridge University Press, 1993.

Biale, David. *Gershom Scholem: Kabbalah and Counterhistory*. Cambridge: Harvard University Press, 1979.

———. *Power and Powerlessness in Jewish History*. New York: Schocken Books, 1987.

———. Review of *Authority, Power and Leadership in the Jewish Polity: Cases and Issues*, by Daniel J. Elazar, ed. *Jewish Political Studies Review*, vol. 5:1–2 (Spring, 1993).

Blidstein, Gerald. *Ekronot Mediniim b'Mishnat Ha-Rambam* [Political Concepts in Maimonidean Halakhah] Israel: Bar Ilan University Press, 1983.

———. "Notes on Hefker Bet Din in Talmudic and Medieval Law." *Dine Israel* 4 (1973).

Breuer, Isaac. *Mein Weg*. Zurich: Morascha Verlag, 1988.

———. *Messiasspuren*. Frankfurt am Main: Verlag Rudolph Leonhard Hammon, 1918.

———. *Moriah*. Jerusalem: Ha-Sifriya l'ma'an Sifrut Haredit ba-Eretz Yisrael, 1954.

———. *Sha'ali Serufah: Zur Erinnerung an das deutsche Judentum*. Jerusalem: Mossad Yitzhak Breuer, 1979.

Breuer. Mordechai. *Jüdische Orthodoxie im Deutschen Reich 1871–1918*. Frankfurt am Main: Judischer Verlag bei Athenäum, 1986.

Carlebach, Joseph. *Das Gesetztreue Judentum*. Berlin: Schocken Verlag, 1936.

Carlebach, Julius. "The Foundations of German-Jewish Orthodoxy, An Interpretation." *Leo Baeck Institute Yearbook*, 33:1988.

Chadwick, Owen. *The Secularization of the European Mind in the Nineteenth Century*. Cambridge: Cambridge University Press, 1977.

Cohen, Hermann. "Der polnische Jude," in *Jüdische Schriften*. 3 vols. Bruno Strauss, ed. Berlin: C. A. Schwetschke & Sohn, 1924.

Cohen, Stuart. "The Concept of The Three *Ketarim*: Its Place in Jewish Political Thought and Its Implications for a Study of Jewish Constitutional History," *AJS Review*, vol. 9:1 (Spring 1984).

Dan, Joseph. ed. *Binah: Studies in Jewish History*. Vol. 1. New York: Praeger, 1989.

Döblin, Alfred. *Journey to Poland*. Translated by Joachim Neugroschel. New York: Paragon House, 1991.

Eisenstadt, S. N. "Intellectuals and Tradition." *Daedalus*, (Spring 1972).

———. "Post-Traditional Societies and the Continuity and Reconstruction of Tradition," *Daedalus*, (Winter 1973).

Elazar, Daniel and Cohen, Stuart. *The Jewish Polity*. Bloomington: Indiana University Press, 1984.

Elazar, Daniel J., ed. *Authority, Power and Leadership in the Jewish Polity*. Lanham, MD: University Press of America, 1991.

———. *Community & Polity: the Organizational Dynamics of American Jewry*. Philadelphia: Jewish Publication Society of America, 1976.

———. "Covenant as the Basis of the Jewish Political Tradition." *The Jewish Journal of Sociology*. Vol. 10:1 (June 1978).

———. *Kinship and Consent: The Political Tradition and Its Contemporary Uses*. Lanham, MD: University Press of America, 1983.

———. *Morality & Power: Contemporary Jewish Views*. Lanham, MD: University Press of America, 1990.

———. *People and Polity: The Organizational Dynamics of World Jewry*. Detroit: Wayne State University Press, 1989.

Elon, Menachem. *Jewish Law: History, Sources, Principles*. 3 vols. Translated by Bernard Auerbach and Melvin Sykes. Philadelphia: Jewish Publication Society, 1994.

Federbusch, Shimon. *Mishpat ha-Melucha b'Yisrael* [The Law of the King in Jewish Law]. Jerusalem: Mossad Ha-Rav Kook, 1973.

Finkelscherer, Herbert. "Die Quellen und Motive der Staats- und Gesellschaftsauffassung des Don Isaak Abravanel," *Monatsschrift fur Geschichte und Wissenschaft des Judentums.* Vol. 81: 1937.

Finkelstein, Louis. *Jewish Self-Government in the Middle Ages.* New York: Jewish Theological Seminary of America, 1924; reprint ed., Westport: Greenwood Press, 1975.

Freeman, Gordon. *The Heavenly Kingdom: Aspects of Political Thought in the Talmud and Midrash.* Lanham, MD: University Press of America, 1986.

Funkenstein, Amos. *Perceptions of Jewish History.* Berkeley: University of California Press, 1993.

Geertz, Clifford. *Local Knowledge.* New York: Basic Books, 1983.

Gellner, Ernest. *Culture, Identity and Politics.* London: Cambridge University Press, 1987.

Gerth, H. H. and C. W. Mills. *From Max Weber.* New York: Oxford University Press, 1978.

Gitelman, Zvi, ed. *The Quest for Utopia: Jewish Political Ideas and Institutions Throughout the Ages.* Armonk, NY: M. E. Sharpe, 1992.

Goldberg, Harvey E., ed. *Judaism Viewed From Within and Without: Anthropological Studies.* Albany: State University of New York Press, 1987.

Graetz, Michael. "From Corporate Community to Ethnic-Religious Minority, 1750–1830." *Leo Baeck Institute Yearbook.* Vol. 37: 1992.

Green, Kenneth Hart. *Jew and Philosopher: The Return to Maimonides in the Jewish Thought of Leo Strauss.* Albany: State University of New York Press, 1993.

Halpern, Ben. *The Idea of the Jewish State.* Cambridge: Harvard University Press, 1969.

Heinemann, Isaac. *Ta'amei Ha-Mitzvot b'Sifrut Yisrael* [The Meaning of the Commandments in Jewish Literature]. 2 vols. Jerusalem: Ha-Histadrut Ha-Zionit, 1966.

Herzl, Theodor. *The Jewish State*. New York: American Zionist Emergency Council, 1946.

Hirsch, Naphtali. *Die Freie Vereinigung für die Interessen des orthodoxen Judentums: eine Beleuchtung ihrer Aufgabe und seitherigen Wirksamkeit*. Frankfurt am Main: Louis Golde, 1903.

Hirsch, Samson Raphael. *Judaism Eternal*, Translated by I. Grunfeld, ed. London: Soncino Press, 1956.

————. *Horeb: A Philosophy of Jewish Laws and Obserances*. Translated by I. Grunfeld. London: Soncino, 1962.

Hobsbawm, Eric and Terence Ranger, eds. *The Invention of Tradition*. Cambridge: Cambridge University Press, 1989.

Horovitz, Mordechai (Markus). *Rabbane Frankfurt* [Frankfurt Rabbis]. Translated by Yehoshua Amir. Jerusalem: Mossad Harav Kook, 1972.

Huntington, Samuel P. "The Change to Change: Modernization, Development, and Politics," *Comparative Politics* 3 (April 1971).

Iggers, Georg G. *The German Conception of History*. Middletown: Wesleyan University Press, 1968.

Jacobson, Wolf. "15 Jahre Agudas Jisroel." *Korrespondenzblatt der Agudas-Jisroel-Jugendorganisation*. Vol. 2:4 (April 1927).

Kant, Immanuel. *Religion Within the Limits of Reason Alone*. Translated by Theodore M. Green and Hoyt H. Hudson. New York: Harper Torchbooks, 1960.

Katz, Jacob. *Out of the Ghetto: The Social Background of Jewish Emancipation 1770–1870*. New York: Schocken Books, 1978.

————. *Tradition and Crisis*. Translated by Bernard Dov Cooperman. New York: New York University Press, 1993.

Kellner, Menachem. *Maimonides on Judaism and the Jewish People*. Albany: State University of New York Press, 1991.

Kracauer, Isadore. *Geschichte der Juden in Frankfurt A.M.* Vol. 2. Frankfurt A.M.: Vorstand der Israelitischen Gemeinde Frankfurt a.M., 1927.

Lamberti, Marjorie. *Jewish Activism in Imperial Germany: The Struggle for Civil Equality.* New Haven: Yale University Press, 1978.

Lederhendler, Eli. *The Road to Modern Jewish Politics: Political Tradition and Political Reconstruction in Tsarist Russia.* New York: Oxford University Press, 1989.

Lerner, Ralph and Muhsin Mahdi, eds. *Medieval Political Philosophy.* New York: The Free Press, 1963.

Levenson, Jon. *Sinai & Zion: An Entry Into the Jewish Bible.* New York: Harper & Row, 1985.

Liberles, Robert. "Emancipation and the Structure of the Jewish Community in the Nineteenth Century." *Leo Baeck Institute Yearbook.* Vol. 31:1986.

——— . *Religious Conflict in Social Context: The Resurgence of Orthodox Judaism in Frankfurt am Main, 1838–1877.* Westport, Greenwood Press, 1985.

Luz, Ehud. *Parallels Meet: Religion and Nationalism in the Early Zionist Movement, 1882–1904.* Translated by Lenn Schramm. Philadelphia: Jewish Publication Society, 1988.

MacIntyre, Alisdaire. "Traditions and Conflicts." *Liberal Education.* Vol. 73:5 (November/December 1987).

Mannheim, Karl. "Conservative Thought." Edited by Kurt Wolff. *From Karl Mannheim.* New York: Oxford University Press, 1971.

——— . *Ideology and Utopia: An Introduction to the Sociology of Knowledge.* Translated by Edward A. Shils and Louis Wirth. New York: Harcourt, Brace & World, 1936.

Medding, Peter Y., ed. *Studies in Contemporary Jewry.* Vol 2. Bloomington: Indiana University Press, 1986.

Mekilta de-Rabbi Ishmael. Translated by Jacob Z. Lauterbach. 3 vols. Philadelphia: Jewish Publication Society of America, 1976.

Mendelsohn, Ezra. *On Modern Jewish Politics*. New York: Oxford University Press, 1993.

Mittleman, Alan. "From Private Rights to Public Good." *Jewish Political Studies Review*. Vol. 5:1–2 (Spring 1993).

————. *Between Kant and Kabbalah*. Albany, State University of New York Press, 1990.

Mosse, George. *German Jews Beyond Judaism*. Bloomington: Indiana University Press and Cincinnati: Hebrew Union College Press, 1985.

Nadav, M. "Pinkas Kahal Frankfurt d'Main." *Kiryat Sefer*. Vol. 31. Jerusalem: Magnes Press, 1955–1956.

Neusner, Jacob. *Rabbinic Political Theory*. Chicago: University of Chicago Press, 1991.

Pelikan, Jaroslav. *The Vindication of Tradition*. New Haven: Yale University Press, 1984.

Penner, Hans H. "Is Phenomenology a Method for the Study of Religion?" *Bucknell Review*. Vol. 18:3 (Winter 1970).

Polish, David. "Rabbinic Views on Kingship: A Study in Jewish Sovereignty." *Jewish Political Studies Review*. Vol. 3:1 and 2 (Spring 1991).

Rabin, Elsa and Friedrich Thieberger, eds. *Jüdisches Fest, Jüdischer Brauch: Ein Sammelwerk*. Berlin: Jüdischer Verlag, 1937.

Raphael, Freddy. "Max Weber and Ancient Judaism." *Leo Baeck Institute Yearbook*. Vol. 18: 1973.

Reichel, Asher. *Iggrot Rabbi Isaac Halevy* [The Letters of Rabbi Isaac Halevy]. Jerusalem: Mossad Ha-Rav Kook, 1972.

Reinharz, Jehuda. *Fatherland or Promised Land: The Dilemma of the German-Jew, 1893–1914*. Ann Arbor: University of Michigan Press, 1975.

Rosenheim, Jacob. *Agudistische Schriften*. Frankfurt am Main: Verlag des Israelit und Hermon, 1929.

————. "Konstituierung des Zentralrates," *Blätter*. Frankfurt am Main: Gruppenverband der Palastina-Zentrale und der Jugend-Organisation der Agudas Jisroel fur Deutschland, 1921.

——— . *Erinnerungen, 1870–1920*. Frankfurt am Main: Waldemar Kramer Verlag, 1970.

——— . *Ohale Jacob: Ausgewählte Aufsätze und Ansprachen*. Frankfurt am Main: J. Kauffmann Verlag, 1930.

Schepansky, Israel. *Ha-Takkanot b'Yisrael* [The Takkanot of Israel]. 4 vols. Jerusalem: Mossad Ha-Rav Kook, 1993.

Schiff, Gary. *Tradition and Politics: The Religious Parties of Israel*. Detroit: Wayne State University Press, 1977.

Schorsch, Ismar. *Jewish Reactions to German Anti-Semitism, 1870–1914*. New York and Philadelphia, Columbia University Press and Jewish Publication Society of America, 1972.

——— . "On the History of the Political Judgment of the Jew," *Leo Baeck Memorial Lecture*. No. 20. New York: Leo Baeck Institute, 1976.

Schwab, Hermann. *The History of Orthodox Jewry in Germany*. Translated by Irene R. Birnbaum. London: The Mitre Press, 1950.

Sharpe, Eric. *Comparative Religion: A History*. LaSalle, IL: Open Court Press, 1986.

Shils, Edward A. *Tradition*. Chicago: University of Chicago Press, 1981.

Sicker, Martin. *The Judaic State: A Study in Rabbinic Political Theory*. New York: Praeger, 1988.

Smith, Donald. *Religion and Political Development*. Boston: Little, Brown & Co., 1970.

Smith, Wilfred Cantwell. *The Meaning and End of Religion*. Minneapolis: Fortress Press, 1991.

Soloveitchik, Haym. "Rupture and Reconstruction: The Transformation of Contemporary Orthodoxy." *TRADITION*. Vol. 28:4, 1994.

Soloveitchik, Joseph. *'Al Ha-Tshuvah* [On Repentance]. Pinchas Peli. ed. Jerusalem: World Zionist Organization, 1974.

Sorkin, David. *The Transformation of German Jewry 1780–1840*. New York: Oxford, 1987.

Spinoza, Benedict. *Chief Works of Benedict de Spinoza*. Translated by R. H. M. Elwes. New York: Dover, 1951.

Statuten der freien Vereinigung für die Interessen des orthodoxen Judentums. Frankfurt am Main: M. Slobotsky, 1886.

Strauss, Leo, ed. *The History of Political Philosophy*. Chicago: University of Chicago Press, 1972.

————. *Philosophy and Law*. Translated by Fred Baumann Philadelphia: Jewish Publication Society, 1987.

————. *What is Political Philosophy?* Chicago: University of Chicago Press, 1988.

Sturm, Douglas. "Corporations, Constitutions and Covenants: On Forms of Human Relation and the Problem of Legitimacy." *Journal of the American Academy of Religion*. Vol. 41, 1973.

Tal, Uriel. *Christians and Jews in Germany: Religion, Politics and Ideology in the Second Reich, 1870–1914*. Translated by Noah Jonathan Jacobs. Ithaca: Cornell University Press, 1975.

Toury, Jacob. *Die politischen Orientierungen der Juden in Deutschland*. Tubingen: J.C.B. Mohr (Paul Siebeck), 1966.

Trend, J. B. and H. Loewe, eds. *Isaak Abravanel*. Cambridge: Cambridge University Press, 1937.

Troeltsch, Ernst. *The Social Teachings of the Christian Churches*. Translated by Olive Wyon. New York: Macmillan, 1931.

Tsur, Yaakov. *Ha-Ortodoxiya Ha-Yehudit b'Germania v'Yachasa l'Hitarganut Ha-Yehudit u'l'Tsiyonnut: 1896–1911.* [German Jewish Orthodoxy and its Attitude Toward Internal Organization and Zionism, 1896–1911]. Ph.D. Diss. Tel Aviv University, 1982.

Twiss, Sumner B. and Walter H. Conser Jr. *Experience of the Sacred*. Hanover: Brown University Press, 1992.

Vital, David. *Zionism: The Crucial Phase*. Oxford: Oxford University Press, 1987.

Weber, Max. *Ancient Judaism*. New York: Free Press, 1952.

———— . *Economy and Society.* Translated by Guenther Roth and Claus Wittich, eds. Berkeley: University of California Press, 1978.

———— . *The Methodology of the Social Sciences.* Translated by Edward A. Shils and Henry A. Finch. Glencoe, IL: The Free Press, 1949.

Weiler, Gershon. *Jewish Theocracy.* Leiden: E. J. Brill, 1988.

Wertheimer, Jack, ed. *The Modern Jewish Experience: A Reader's Guide.* New York: New York University Press, 1993.

———— . *Unwanted Strangers.* New York: Oxford University Press, 1987.

Zahavy, Y. Tsvi. *Me'Hatam Sofer v'ad-Herzl* [From the Hatam Sofer to Herzl] Jerusalem: The Zionist Library of the Zionist Organization, 1972.

Zenner, Walter P., ed. *Persistence and Flexibility: Anthropological Perspectives on the American Jewish Experience.* Albany: State University of New York Press, 1988.

INDEX